MEDINA

Mary McCarthy

MEDINA

HARCOURT BRACE JOVANOVICH, INC., NEW YORK

Originally published, in different form, in *The New Yorker*

ACKNOWLEDGMENTS

My thanks to members of the press corps covering the Medina court-martial, in particular to Sunde Smith (Newsweek), Michael McGovern (New York Daily News), and Kathryn Johnson (AP) for their generosity in offering information and hospitality to a newcomer, but also to Joseph Kane (Time), Kenneth Reich (Los Angeles Times), Homer Bigart (New York Times), Phil Galey (Atlanta Constitution) for joint and individual kindnesses. My appreciation too of the help given by Millie Burchardt, the very pleasant Press Officer in charge. Finally I want to thank James T. Farrell and Cleo Paturos, great newspaper-readers, for clipping and mailing me a diversity of stories on the trial.

MEDINA

cession of character witnesses swearing that he was a dedicated conscientious officer, the press and courtroom spectators had reached a verdict, which was simply that the trial was boring, a waste of time.

That seemed to be the view, too, of the defendant and his counsel, who yawned, stretched, doodled, slumped, whispered, rolled martyrs' eyes skyward, nudged neighboring ribs, cupped mouths to pass sardonic asides, like a pewful of restless schoolboys during a particularly dull and long-drawn-out chapel service. At the defense table, there were big boyish grins of anticipation whenever F. Lee Bailey, the chief civilian defense counsel, rose, shaking off his ennui and settling his collar, to make one of his "innocent" interventions, like the school bad boy, plump and feigning stupidity, who rises to ask a loaded and deferential question: "Sir!"

On the dais at the rear sat the jury—two full colonels, two lieutenant colonels, and a major—in diverse states of glassy fixity or open drowsiness. At the left end, Lt. Col. Bobby Berryhill, Jr., from Decatur, Georgia, double-chinned, pendulous, with large soft brown eyes and a long nose, napped from time to time but when fully awake seemed the most reflective of the jurors and finally, at the close of the testimony, asked the only penetrating questions put to Medina at any point in the trial. At the other end of the dais, the youngest member, Major Dudley L. Budrich, from Chicago, an airborne ranger, blond, with bangs and weakly drawn cowboy features, sucked his hollow cheek in a rhythmic motion or chewed on a wad of gum and yawned in the same steady cadence, his jaws opening and shutting on their hinges, like a machine beating time. In the center, the foreman, Col. William Proctor, from Dunwoody,

5

Georgia, wore an unchanging ferocious glare of command behind accusatory glasses, as though compelling the evidence to present arms and salute him. On his left, a black officer, Lt. Col. Clarence Cooke, born in Enterprise, Alabama, leaned back in his chair and looked indulgent, an adult overseeing a child's game. On the foreman's right, Col. Robert E. Nelson, Jr., originally from Eatontown, Georgia, a thin rather handsome blond officer with cold blue eyes, listened with a curling ironic smile that seemed to mark at least a sarcastic attention to the evidence, but newsmen said it was only a facial tic—the result of combat wounds he suffered in the Korean War. Opposite the jury, behind the spectators' seats, the courtroom door was guarded by a young M.P. sitting on a straight chair and generally asleep.

Facing the jury, the prosecution team—Major William G. Eckhardt and his second, Capt. Franklin R. Wurtzel—assigned by the Army to try the case, presented a façade of severity and grim determination. It was the third of the My Lai 4 cases they had prosecuted, and the third they were going to lose, quite evidently. They acted like the lower end of the batting order with two strikes on them and making blustering motions in the box. Or like members of a freshman debating squad assigned to the less popular side of some already lifeless proposition, such as "RESOLVED, that the United States should withdraw from the Kellogg-Briand Pact." Wurtzel was small, slight, and plaintive, with a breathy lisping voice; Eckhardt, tall and loosely hung, held a big meerschaum pipe in the form of a turbaned Turk's head clamped between his teeth and seemed most in his element when administering the oath to witnesses, which he did with great belligerence and in a voice of thunder.

This forcible-feeble pair had a certain ingenuous pathos. Despite their familiarity (one would think) by this time with the My Lai matter, they appeared poorly prepared and were repeatedly taken by surprise by their own witnesses, as well as scolded, guided, and corrected by the judge.

At the long defense table, opposite the judge, were Medina and his two military lawyers, plus Bailey and two rather indistinct members of his law firm, whose chief function seemed to be errand-running. Each time they left the room or returned, it had to be inserted in the record, interrupting the proceedings and giving an air of busyness and humming activity to the defense organization. But Bailey treated everybody as an errand boy ("Capt. Kadish, make the necessary phone"), scarcely stopping short of the judge. His military associate, Mark Kadish, a young lawyer from Brooklyn doing his hitch in the Army, was dark, with a bright eye like a chicken's, soft whitish arms in summer short-sleeved military shirt, and a rather matronly spread of the hips; when not conferring with Medina or making the necessary phone, he sat with folded arms and head tilted back against the wall, stifling yawns if Eckhardt was examining and looking lazily derisive, like a Jewish intellectual drafted into attendance at some cow college. This appearance was deceptive. The assistant military counsel was Capt. John R. Truman, of Independence, Missouri, also doing his hitch in the Army and a grandnephew of the former President. He smiled a good deal, in a thin eager scholarly way, but otherwise contributed little to the defense presentation and appeared shy.

The judge, Col. Kenneth Howard, was another Georgian and a Methodist Sunday-school teacher. Under his baggy black gown, he wore, not a uniform, but a dark suit, white shirt, and a small flowing black tie, and this rather old-fashioned costume distinguished him from the jury in military dress with the obligatory medals and decorations and from military counsel. Mrs. Millie Burchardt, the civilian press officer, said that he prayed for light before every session. Unlike the other participants, he seemed indeed a prayerful man, guided by the conviction that he was presiding over something more than a legal farce or dutiful debating exercise with a foregone conclusion. He was short, round, slow-spoken, with pepper-and-salt hair that matched his sharp dry country wit, often called into exercise by the theatrics of F. Lee Bailey. Although capable of amusement and drollery, he was also capable of sternness at unseemly laughter in the courtroom. He appeared to know less law than Bailey (*e.g.*, it did not sound as if he had a very sure grasp of the differences between testimonial immunity and transactional immunity) and not to be troubled by it. In making his decisions, he would patiently fall back on common sense, dismissing with a wave of his short broad hand the large green books of case material from which Bailey would cite rules and precedents.

Finally, though, he was moved to anger. More and more, as the trial went on, Bailey, hoping (it was said) for a mistrial if he did not secure an acquittal, goaded him as though sensing a weak point and finally, by repeated pressure, locating it. On September 15, the judge flew off the handle: "Don't repeat back to me that the judge is an idiot and doesn't know what he's doing!" This was what Bailey wanted. There was a long argument behind closed doors, which ended with Judge Howard, doubtless repentant of his outburst, reversing a ruling he had

8

made. But by this time the trial was stumbling anyhow to a close. The prosecution had lost its two principal witnesses and been betrayed by a third. Nobody, even those who believed in Medina's guilt, believed there was any chance of his conviction. Two days later, the judge reduced the additional charge to manslaughter.

Col. Howard's weak point, so insistently probed, may have been his professional pride. Courtroom gossips reported that he felt competitive with Col. Kennedy, who had tried the Calley case. So far as one can tell in the absence of a transcript (no official transcript of either trial is available to the public), Col. Howard had no reason, except his evident modesty, to fear that his performance ranked below Reid Kennedy's; rather the contrary, to guess from published bits. But though "competitive" may not be the word for the judge's state of mind, modesty, combined with a desire to do what is right, can make a mild man sensitive to comparisons. And however Col. Howard stacked up against Col. Kennedy, the Medina trial could not stand comparison with the Calley trial.

This was quickly manifest in the attendance. The military courtroom (always described in the newspapers as "small, stuffy" or "tiny, stuffy") had room for only forty-three people in the spectator section, and the press officers handling the trial expected problems. By court order, thirty seats were provided for the press and four for the public—not counting Mrs. Medina and counsels' wives. Priority would be given to reporters for the networks and wire services, the big dailies, *Time, Newsweek*, three courtroom artists in the front row, the local press. To take care of the press, two overflow rooms were set up, with forty-seven headphones, in the Press Center, and a system of drawing for courtroom passes every morning at 8:30 sharp. If the *Daily News* or CBS man did not show up on time, his seat went into the pool. But as it turned out, the big press hall with desks, telephones, and typewriters was usually half empty, and there were plenty of spare passes in the press officer's basket. Some of the media people who were expected did not materialize; some looked in for a day or so and then dropped out. The German weekly *Der Spiegel* installed a telephone and never came, and you could use the *Spiegel* phone to call a Yellow cab from downtown Atlanta. In the courtroom, filling the unclaimed seats of newsmen, were officers' towheaded children, officers' wives and sisters-in-law, an occasional G.I., one day a Delta Air Lines hostess, and nearly every day a tall curly-haired young major with a drawing-board sketching the principals—he was a research doctor doing his military service and an amateur artist of some talent. The overflow press rooms were used by reporters as hideaways, especially after lunch: it was possible to sleep there, turning off the headphones, and also to smoke, despite a "No Smoking" sign and the intermittent slumbrous presence of an M.P., who was supposed to be on guard.

Word had got around fast that this trial was a dud compared to the Calley trial. "The once lurid testimony seemed stale," Homer Bigart wrote in the New York *Times* during the first week. The Medina show was a box-office turkey. There was no Aubrey Daniel, to put it mildly, in the prosecutor's role. There were no drinking parties with the judge or lawyers or defendant. Medina, small, slit-eyed, looking like the bad Indian in a Western, lacked the all-American appeal of Rusty Calley. The only star was the rather tarnished F. Lee Bailey, in his pin-striped suits, giving desultory interviews on the sidewalk—a benefit performance for the TV crews and photographers stationed in a sort of bandstand outside the courthouse in the punishing sun. In his low uninflected voice, talking into the extended mikes and to a circle of scribbling reporters, he obligingly played to the gallery, promising to call Calley as a defense witness and confront him with startling, hitherto-undisclosed evidence, threatening to bring the White House into the case—a feint he made three times, with aplomb, as though he had Richard M. Nixon up his conjuror's sleeve, like the handkerchief he sometimes slowly drew out in the courtroom and gently shook open. Calley, in fact, was produced, under guard, but the White House, like *Der Spiegel,* ignored Bailey and his client.

The disgusted conviction that the Medina court-martial was a poor road show of the Calley hit was perhaps understandable in the circumstances, given the human appetite for novelty and the fact that a courtroom is a natural stage set on which some sort of drama is expected to emerge. No doubt, too, there was something peculiarly American in the general disappointment, as though a public event that did not "top" a previous one was a drag, a loser, a cheat. "We've heard it before. Why bore us?" was the sullen refrain, though it is hard to see how the Medina trial, even if well conducted by the prosecution, could have failed to be in many respects a repetition of the Calley trial. There was the same personnel, returning to tell its story again, the same bodies on the trail and in the ditch. What did the press and public want—mint-fresh atrocities, in preference to stale ones?

The feeling of boredom and futility at Fort McPherson was aggravated by the fact that concurrently at Fort Meade, Maryland, still another road show was performing—the trial of Col. Henderson, with again the same basic cast of characters: the men of Charlie Company, Lt. LaCrosse, Lt. Alaux (artillery), the helicopter pilots Thompson and Colburn, Millians and Culverhouse, the task-force officer Major Calhoun, Major Watke, Col. Luper, and, hovering up in the flies, the *deus ex machina* and chief author of My Lai, Col. Frank Barker, well beyond the reach of the law's long arm, having answered a higher summons three months after My Lai, when he died in a helicopter crash. There was a growing and eerie familiarity about these men, some still in uniform, some not, making their entrances and exits, like members of an all-male stock company, sometimes cast in slightly different parts: a character witness in the Medina trial would be a prosecution witness in the trial of Col. Henderson. You recognized quite a few from their photos in the various books on My Lai and Calley, on sale at national airports; some had changed their appearance, let hair or sideburns grow, added a mustache, making you feel doubly that they were actors in different make-ups.

While waiting, paper cup of coffee and Army doughnut in hand, for the day's testimony in the Medina trial to begin, reporters could look through the morning paper with yesterday's testimony from the Henderson trial. Far fields seemed greener. Their testimony at Fort Meade sounded better than *our* testimony. Why didn't we have Charles West, since they did? How did *their* prosecutor get those tapes (made for his own amusement by Capt. Lewellen, of the radio dialogue that accompanied the My Lai action), which haven't been played here, for us? (In fact, the tapes were finally introduced into evidence in the Fort McPherson courtroom, but by the defense, rather than the prosecution.) Witnesses were shuttling back and forth between Fort Meade and Fort Mac. At one point, when F. Lee Bailey was announcing Col. Henderson as a defense witness, it looked as if the two trials might homogenize into a single cloudy mixture, which at least would have cut costs to the taxpayer. In the end, Col. Henderson was not brought to the stand in the Medina case, but, nearly two months after his own acquittal, Medina took the stand in the Henderson case, as a defense witness.

Before Calley was arraigned, some of the younger lawyers in JAG (the Judge Advocate General's office) proposed holding a mass trial on the Nuremberg pattern, with all the suspects in the dock together, from Gen. Koster (never brought to the bar, but censured), down to Staff Sgt. Mitchell (acquitted at Fort Hood, Texas) and Sgt. Hutto (acquitted at Fort Mc-Pherson)—a clean sweep. The idea was vetoed, but it might have satisfied, at least visually, a desire for even-handed justice, avoided repetitiousness, and apportioned blame in large, small, and medium slices according to a single measure. The method used, of holding separate trials, with separate juries, combined with high-level administrative decisions to absolve some of the parties without trial, was bound to produce a haphazard result and leave a sense of unfairness. My Lai was a single big crime, committed by many parties, with accessories before and after the fact; whether Lt. Calley was more or less guilty than Gen. Koster need not have been left to the public, in the throes of hysteria and, finally, indifference, to decide.

The Medina trial, theoretically, had an advantage over the Calley trial, in that the whole picture was laid out more clearly than in the Calley case, where the focus was on the ground, on

the erratic character and behavior of a single malformed lieutenant who, though not demented in the legal sense, was plainly
unable to function in the Army or in American society, even
though in his strivings and failure to "make it," he appeared
more horribly typical than, say, his prosecutor, Capt. Aubrey
Daniel. Since he showed no other signs of sadistic inclination,
his conduct at My Lai defies understanding unless it is seen
as an effort to distinguish himself, win credit—an all-out spurt
in a success-drive. Calley both got the point and missed it about
Vietnam.

In the Medina trial Calley and the first platoon figured small,
for the most part out of sight, in another part of the village;
without the distorting bent of his personality the massacre
can be centered in a wider frame. If you imagine My Lai 4
as a picture, the top layer, at 2,000 feet, is occupied by Gen.
Koster (code name Saber 6) in his helicopter; below him, in
his helicopter, at 1,500 feet, is Col. Henderson (code name
Rawhide 6), the brigade officer; the next layer is occupied by
Lt. Col. Barker (code name Coyote 6) in the command-control
ship, ranging over the whole operation, his brain child, at a
general altitude of 1,000 feet—the unit he has combined to
put it into execution is christened after him: Task Force Barker.
Underneath him are OH 1b gunships, and occupying the lowest
stratum, in a small observation craft, an OH 23 or "bubble
ship," are Hugh Thompson and Larry Colburn. On the ground,
having been airlifted in, preceded by gunship fire and an
artillery "prep" of the village, are Capt. Medina and his command group, in the rice field; Medina is standing on a grave
mound. Proceeding or soon to proceed into the village itself
are Lt. Brooks (deceased), Lt. Calley, the first and second

platoons, Haeberle, a photographer, and Roberts, an Army writer. The third platoon, Lt. Alaux, and the mortar unit have stayed behind, for the present, with Medina. Phu, an interpreter, is there too, to be joined later by Minh, another interpreter and interrogation expert. Also on the ground are the villagers, some eating breakfast. The time is about 7:30.

The helicopters, large and small, rotating above in hierarchical stratification, have a bird's-eye view of the "combat assault"; that, in fact, is what they are there for. What Gen. Koster saw is not known. Col. Henderson denied seeing anything from his air-lane that he could interpret as unusual, and indeed, in his trial, there was much dispute as to his altitude, the prosecution placing him low and the defense, naturally, high—above Gen. Koster.

Soon, though, Thompson and Colburn do see something unusual, circle back, hover, and land—several times. In the gunships, Millians, Culverhouse, and Brian Livingston also discern something wrong. Higher up, in the command helicopters, the regular counterclockwise movement is disturbed, and there seem to be shifts in position. Is this because of the alarm raised by Thompson over his radio or are the ships simply returning to base to refuel?

Back at LZ Dottie, the take-off point and Tactical Operations Center, are dark, bony, hawk-nosed Major Calhoun and pale stout Capt. Kotouc, the F-2 or brigade intelligence officer (acquitted at Fort Mac of assaulting and maiming a prisoner by cutting off his thumb; the charge had been reduced from murder). He is responsible for the faulty intelligence that supposedly has prepared the ground for the massacre: *i.e.*, that Charlie Company would find the 48th VC Battalion in the village and that at seven o'clock that morning all the women and children would have gone to market in the town.

At least once, Major Calhoun leaves LZ Dottie and flies over My Lai 4. Col. Barker, at least once, returns to LZ Dottie and talks to Major Watke, the helicopter command officer, in the TOC. Col. Henderson is in and out of the TOC and, according to one witness, lands at the My Lai 4 hamlet, carrying a clipboard, and speaks angrily to Capt. Medina. It is at the time of the Carter Medivac, and a black, SP4 Gerald Heming, a demolitions man attached to the command group, watches two helicopters alight; one is the dust-off (medical evacuation) chopper, and the other contains Col. Henderson, who gets out and tells Medina something like "These killings have to stop." But this witness loses credibility with the jury on several counts: he is wearing an Afro beard and a fuschia-and-gold dashiki with a heart pattern, which stand out like a private fantasy against the regulation summer tans and clean shaves of counsel and M.P.'s; he confuses the gold leaf worn by Major Budrich of the jury with a colonel's silver eagle; he has been drinking (four quarts of wine before a chat with Capt. Kadish the previous night, and some more on top of that); he has tried LSD; and he has a high wild screechy equalitarian sense of humor ("How did you recognize Col. Henderson? Did you ever speak to him?" "No." "Then how do you know him as Col. Henderson?" "I see him every morning at the base. He is coming out of *his* hootch, and I am coming out of *my* hootch").

The tall angry officer with the clipboard, sometimes descending from a helicopter, was one of the mysteries of the trial. He appeared several times in the testimony, assuming different forms, like a god in metamorphosis. Sometimes he seemed to be Major Calhoun; a logical guess was Col. Barker. But there is nothing in the record to show that Barker or Calhoun ever landed at My Lai 4. He can scarcely have been Gen. Koster, aloft, at the apex of the action. It is as if, in the reveries of Charlie Company, some such officer *ought* to have appeared from the skies, a stern and righteous commander zeroing in like a thunderbolt to put a stop to the murder orgy.

That dream officer, Moses from Sinai, should of course have been Col. Barker. He was in command; quite early, while airborne, he got (or overheard) word from the bubble ship that civilians were being killed indiscriminately. He seems to have handled this routinely with a transmission to Major Calhoun, asking him to relay the message to Medina. Yet according to Medina's testimony, Col. Barker was in direct touch all along with him, full of eager queries about the VC body count. And another witness described seeing the C-and-C ship hovering low at the far end of the hamlet. A different version says that it was Watke, not Barker, who alerted Calhoun, if alerted is the right word, as well as Barker himself and then, perhaps because no action was taken, Col. Henderson and Gen. Koster. Still another story is that Barker radioed the TOC that he had had a complaint from "higher up"—just as though this was the first he had heard of anything untoward. Meanwhile Thompson in person was at LZ Dottie, reiterating his complaint and pleading that something be done. It must have been around this time that a witness saw Major Watke in the TOC talking angrily to Major Calhoun. Still no action; merely a transmission from Calhoun to Medina hoping that no civilians were getting hurt. No doubt Barker was already composing his official report on the operation as he cruised over the scene: ". . . well planned, well executed, and successful. Friendly casualties were light and the enemy suffered heavily." He gave a KIA count of 128 VC, noted eleven CIA (VC captured in action), and three captured weapons (old American rifles).

These figures included Alpha and Bravo Companies. To Charlie Company, out of the over-all total, he assigned fifteen KIA, all three captured weapons, and one U.S. wounded—Pfc. Carter, who had shot himself in the foot. In reply, Gen. Westmoreland sent his commendations: "Congratulations on the operation for Task Force Barker to officers and men of C-1-2 [Charlie Company] for outstanding action." But you did not need to be a four-star general to read between the lines of Col. Barker's summary: only three weapons captured, with a KIA count of 128 and a CIA of eleven? Then at least 125 unarmed persons must have been killed. Who or what were they? Barker's figures were prima-facie evidence of a wholesale murder of civilians, legible to anybody as calling for an investigation. Instead, Gen. Westmoreland's message had the effect of closing the subject with a snap. John Paul, Medina's radio operator: ". . . we did hear that we were under investigation, but a few days later I heard—this was just a rumor—that Gen. Westmoreland had given us a job-well-done, and it was dropped."

At the time Barker got his job-well-done from the general, stories of the murders were circulating, not only among the troops, but also among local Vietnamese government authorities—already, that same afternoon, the tale was being spread by survivors. Probably fearing that some of this unpleasant publicity might have percolated upward, Barker tried in guarded language to take care of the question. Without citing figures, he spoke of "a problem in population control and medical care of those civilians caught in the fires of opposing forces." As he knew by then, if he had not known all along, there had been no cross fire at My Lai 4.

The mystery of how Barker had arrived at his body count only deepened at Fort McPherson, when Medina agreed that he had given the task force commander a KIA figure of sixty-nine for Calley's platoon, fourteen from gunship fire, and one from an unidentified cause—a total of eighty-four. In reducing Medina's KIA to fifteen, Barker perhaps hoped to draw attention away from the activities of Charlie Company.

IN THE MEDINA TRIAL, none of the existing mysteries was cleared up and others were created. Why were witnesses who had strongly inculpated Medina in earlier appearances not called to the stand here? Gary Crossley ("We phoned Medina and told him what the circumstances were [nothing but women and children in the hamlet], and he said just keep going"), Paul Meadlo ("I don't know if the CO gave the order to kill or not, but he was right there when it happened"), Herbert Carter, Charles West, the writer Jay Roberts. Perhaps Eckhardt tried and could not persuade them to testify again; perhaps he mistrusted them and feared they might change their stories. Yet the prosecution did produce one unwilling witness, who came and took the Fifth Amendment, and a number of others who let the side down. Why call Policeman Louis Martin, whose testimony was obviously shaky and who broke down, when the defense got at him, and admitted to having fantasies, and draw the line at the combat correspondent Jay Roberts, who was heard at

Fort Meade and who in the Calley trial was sure that Medina spent two hours in the village—testimony which, if believed, would utterly destroy his alibi?

At Fort McPherson, trails opened by the prosecution would quickly be abandoned, as though it was too much work to hack a way through the contradictions. Instead, an overgrowth of confusion sprang up. Wurtzel's shoulders slumped as he relinquished an unforthcoming witness; Eckhardt turned on his heel. With the multiple references to a running child being shot, you never knew which one was meant, and were there not two but three? Not counting, of course, those shot by Calley and the first platoon.

There were many short recesses, including one when the prosecutor's wife had a baby and one when Col. Nelson of the jury had a death in the family. The short recesses suggested fatigue symptoms: "Let's take a break." It was an over-all fatigue, due not to courtroom pressures (the schedule was light) or the August and early September heat, but to weariness of the subject and the issues. The issues faded, like much-washed dirty linen, and more and more the trial turned on technicalities. On the admissibility of hearsay evidence (allowable as a statement against interest or as leading to an action), on testimonial versus transactional immunity for witnesses pleading the Fifth Amendment (the first offers a witness immunity from prosecution for anything he may *say* on the stand; the second is supposed to cover him for the whole transaction, before, during, and after his testimony), on the admissibility of statements made to a lie-detector expert (ruled allowable) as distinguished from lie-detector findings (not allowable). Over and over, the jury filed out while counsel and the judge argued about points of law.

Obviously points of law have their place in a law court, but here wrangling and bickering over them seemed to be taking more than double the man-hours given to the actual testimony and to require more and longer recesses as the judge pondered them in chambers. Col. Howard's patience created impatience around him.

On points of fact there were similar long and useless contentions. Two Vietnamese interpreters gave depositions for the prosecution in South Vietnam, the GRVN having denied them passports to come to the U.S. and testify. First of all, the defense charged that as a matter of fact the U.S. government had not used all available pressure on the Thieu government to compel the presence of the witnesses in court. The judge said he thought the government had acted in good faith. Bailey, striking an injured pose, announced that he would call for Nixon's personal intervention to fetch them (Judge Howard, amused: "I don't know the number of the White House. Do you?"). The defense evidently hoped to have the depositions thrown out, or, failing that, to leave the inference to be drawn that the prosecution had its reasons for not wanting Sergeants Minh and Phu in court. To give Nixon and Rogers time to exercise due pressure on Thieu and also for another reason, having to do with a contempt citation, the court decreed a ten-day recess, which included Labor Day. When the sessions resumed, though nothing had changed, Bailey did not press his objections. Minh's and Phu's depositions were heard.

But not before another wrangle lasting several hours. In their depositions, both Minh and Phu agreed that Minh had asked Capt. Medina, "Why we kill everybody in hamlet and burn all hootches and kill animals?" Or words to that effect. To which Medina had answered something like "Orders" or "That was an order" or "He just carrying out an order." Before the tapes could be heard by the jury, Bailey played a new card. The depositions were inadmissible because there was no clear indication that either man understood English. Laughter in the court. The idea that an ARVN sergeant, graduate of an interpreters' school, did not know even simple English appealed to the Army sense of humor. As the tapes showed, the defense team had already been ugly with the witnesses during the taking of the depositions: in his questions, Capt. Kadish made clear his opinion that Minh, being Vietnamese, would not know the truth from a lie. And to Phu, Kadish: "Do you *know* north from south?" Aside from providing some Caucasian entertainment, Bailey's ploy was a gross waste of the court's time. It was plain that the interpreters knew enough English to recognize the primary word "orders." But the judge sent the jury out, listened to the tapes of the depositions, and came up with "a finding of fact," namely, that "this witness [Minh] on March 16, 1968, could speak English."

PHU, WHO WAS the Charlie Company interpreter, went on with the troops when they finally left the hamlet. He testified that in the afternoon they met some civilians in a hamlet fifteen or twenty kilometers away and that Capt. Medina instructed him to tell them to move out. If they were still there "when we go on operation here again . . . they get killed, same like people in last village." Little attention was paid by either side to this part of his evidence, with its implication that Medina did know exactly what had been going on in My Lai 4. But it implied something else as well, something so taken for granted by both sides that whenever it came up, it passed unnoticed: the policy of creating refugees. The deliberate creation of refugees is not regarded by the United States as a war crime, and Medina was not being tried for it. In fact, generating refugees was treated by the court and by the witnesses as completely natural and normal, in contrast to the actions cited in the indictment, which even when felt to be defensible seemed to need excuse as representing a deviation from the usual standards of conduct. In Vietnam, murder of non-combatants and assaults on prisoners, however often they occurred, were not "policy."

The tranquil acceptance of organized brutality by the Army was laid bare with simple candor by Medina as he gave his opening testimony on his briefing of his men the night of March 15. Here and in the Calley trial, testimony had varied as to whether or not he had ordered non-combatants killed (" '. . . destroy everything that moved,' " Martin; " '. . . kill everything in the village that moved,' " Flynn; " '. . . kill everything in the village,' " Stanley; " '. . . kill everything that breathed,' " Lamartina; " '. . . leave nothing living in the area except GI's,' " Kinch; whereas others said that there had been no mention of killing anything but livestock).

At Fort McPherson, Medina was very much at ease as he expanded on the briefing, recollecting the scene with the men gathered around him seated on ammunition bunkers as he drew a map on the sand. "I told them that we had permission, Col. Barker had received permission from the ARVNs, that the village could be destroyed since it was a VC stronghold, to burn the houses down, to kill all the livestock, to cut any of the crops that might feed VC, to cave in the wells and destroy the village. . . .

"I had two questions that I recall being asked. One was, do we shoot women and children? My answer to that was no, use your common sense; you don't shoot women and children. If the individual is trying to hurt you and has a weapon, then you can shoot him. If he is evading and does not stop, fire your warning shot. If he doesn't stop then, you can either fire to wound or to kill the individual.

"The other question was in reference to closing the wells. One individual thought it would be a good idea if we could obtain some poison to poison the water. I told him that we didn't do this, that we didn't want to poison the water supply. . . . I told them just to close the wells by caving in the walls or contaminating them by cutting a banana stalk and putting it in the well." He is sure the story reflects credit on him—patient, fatherly, setting an example of restraint. Above all, *moderate.* He was the same in the field, the next day, when he was eating lunch in the schoolhouse, which had not yet been blown up, with two little Vietnamese girls he had found ("He was feeding them and treating them real nice," Sgt. Calvin Hawkins, a demolitions man). Then, after the meal, he sent them "on their way" (his expression) to Quang Ngai or Son Tinh in the company of an old man, *i.e.*, to an orphanage or, more likely, a refugee camp.

It seems improbable that this wary company commander actually ordered the murder of civilians with 105 juveniles listening, though the tenor of the briefing can be imagined from the fact that it gave rise irrepressibly to the question "Do we kill women and children?" The men were to murder a hamlet; on that point, the instructions were clear. A veil was drawn as to what was to become of the population. They were to be disregarded, just as though they did not exist. The next step, to conduct them from virtual to real non-existence, then became easy.

If this is reflected on, some of the mystery surrounding My Lai may resolve. Starting with the puzzle of why Charlie Company, under-strength, with 105 combat-green troops, was sent in to attack a VC battalion estimated to consist of 250 to 280 men, when the usual ratio considered acceptable by the Army for an assault on a fortified position was two or three U.S. to one enemy. No explanation has ever been vouchsafed by the Army for such a departure from policy, and the silence permits one to theorize that those conducting the operation did *not* expect to find the 48th VC in the hamlet. But then what was the point of the attack?

Assume that the grand design was the physical elimination of the whole network of hamlets and sub-hamlets known as Pinkville, long a VC haven, and assume that the intelligence was the *reverse* of what has been claimed, *i.e.*, that the 48th VC had *withdrawn* from the area, probably for rest and recuperation in the mountains near the Laotian border, leaving behind perhaps a few local guerrillas, who would run away when the troops swept through. The purpose of the action would be to profit from the occasion to dry up the ocean in which the VC fish swam, that is, the peasantry. When the VC units returned, Pinkville in its entirety would be KIA, with not a living soul left to collaborate, not an animal or a grain of rice. The people, if they constituted a problem (tried to "evade"), could be shot;

otherwise they would be told to "move on" to the cities, as refugees.

Of course this would not be the first or the last operation designed on a counter-Maoist principle, to deprive the enemy of his base in the native population and generate a flow of refugees. But in most cases refugees were either generated "accidentally," by aerial bombing or artillery exchanges, or, when forcibly removed by the Army into camps, as in the famous clearing out of the Iron Triangle in 1967, treated with some slight deference to humanitarian concepts—the peasants were allowed to bring food, animals, bedding, utensils, and so on, into the camps prepared for them. What stands out in My Lai 4 is that no provision of any kind was made for the people.

Unusual secrecy, too, surrounded the operation. Medina said this was because of the fear of leaks through the always-unreliable ARVN: the 48th VC might be tipped off and steal away. But if the 48th VC was known to have already withdrawn, other motives for secrecy can be presumed. Col. Barker had permission from the district or province chief—Medina was not sure which—to destroy the hamlet, but this depended no doubt on the supposition that it contained an enemy force. GRVN authorities were not always happy to issue these destruction permits to the Americans, and it would have been rare, if not unheard-of, to give one to "sanitize" an area of mere sympathizers. Had news leaked that a combat assault was being prepared on the My Lai complex, embarrassment might have been created for Task Force Barker. We do not know *when* Col. Barker got his permission; it may have been weeks old, dating from a time when a VC battalion was really based (or believed to be based) in My Lai 4.

The uncommonly vigorous and bitter reaction of the district chief to the atrocity suggests that he perceived that he (or his superior) had been tricked by the Americans. Both this man, an ARVN lieutenant, and the village chief made repeated reports, with figures, of the known dead (440 for the Son My area), so categorical and, in the lieutenant's case, fiery in tone that an American advisor supposed that ". . . it was. a VC chief, the one who reported it. . . ."

If we assume that intelligence of a VC withdrawal gave Barker a long-desired opportunity to move swiftly to clean out Pinkville, it does not seem too farfetched. The whole operation bears the mark of a particular personality, outstanding in an army that was not noted for enterprise, and which corresponds to Medina's description of the Task Force commander—"a very Gung Ho, Special Forces type of officer."

Capt. Kotouc concurred: "Col. Barker planned operations like artillery people talk about targets of opportunity. He operated fast." Besides, the thrill of risk—for the intelligence might have been mistaken—was likely to attract Barker, a former parachute jumper, and, to cite Medina again, "a hard charger."

It is not necessary to think that Barker's program included a massacre of civilians. Perhaps he really believed that a majority of the women and children would have gone to market that morning. Or he *hoped* Kotouc's intelligence on this point was right. And it was important to him and Medina that the men believe it. Of course the old and the sick would be in the hamlet, but this was not mentioned. They would object to the killing of their animals and the burning of their houses and food stocks. Hence "incidents," at the very minimum, could

27

be counted on to occur, unless strong instructions were given to the contrary, and a close supervision exercised.

As far as one can tell from Medina's behavior, the only instruction given him had to do with speed. On the radio and in person, he kept urging his men to hurry up, get on with it, as though he had been ordered to work fast and clear out of there before anybody caught him. This may help explain the fact, repeatedly elicited by Prosecutor Eckhardt, that no medical aid was given to any wounded or dying civilians Medina saw in the course of his rounds that morning. The *only* medical aid given in My Lai 4 was to Pfc. Carter, whose foot was treated before he was medivacked out at about 11:00 A.M.

"No medical aid given," "No medical given," "No, sir, no medical aid," the toneless witnesses all agreed. This was confirmed by Medina, who admitted to having seen thirty-five or more bodies, not counting those he shot himself or saw shot. When pressed to account for this astonishing circumstance, he said he assumed they were all dead, without bothering to check. When he saw the child shot—by mistake, as he claimed—he said to his men, "Let's get out of here," evincing that same strange hurry and forestalling any intervention by the command-group medic. The same with the woman of Charge 1. And yet, as he said himself, "I have given aid to wounded VCs many times." If he was accustomed to treating wounded *enemy*, what, unless an order, could have caused him to withhold treatment from wounded *civilians?*

Aside from the bodies, dead or dying, that he actually saw, there were the complaints of the helicopter crewmen, which, according to his testimony, did not reach him till between 10:30 and 11:00 A.M. Whether this is believed or not, he did get a report from Calley between 7:30 and 9:30, telling him that a helicopter pilot had landed and objected to the way Calley was running his platoon. Medina did not ask what the pilot had not liked, any more than he went himself or sent a medic to investigate after receiving the later report.

Yet, as the court learned from Chief Warrant Officer Thompson's testimony, not all the bodies heaped up and lying about were dead. He found some still alive and medivacked them on his own initiative to Quang Ngai City. Medina's striking lack of curiosity, not to say his callousness, might have had some excuse had the action been contested, had his medics been busy caring for U.S. wounded and dying. There was no shortage of pharmaceuticals: as one medic related, the company had learned at the briefing that they would get extra morphine and ten Syrettes more than they usually carried. In the circumstances one can only guess that Medina, by withholding aid, was obeying an instruction not to let himself be distracted by the population, should any get in the way. He had emphasized in his briefing that this was a vengeance operation for the buddies lost by Charlie Company to snipers, booby traps, and mines, and to sustain that mood in the men, keep them jacked up (his expression), it was important that the commander not show softness toward enemy sympathizers whose homes were being systematically "wasted."

Such a phrase as "Get rid of him," pronounced by Medina of the blind-and-deaf old man in the burning hootch, summed up with precision the orders of the day. Medina explained that his men had misconstrued him: he only meant to get the old man out of the way. But getting rid of the population (a phrase that may well have occurred in his briefing) implied a similar in-

29

difference to the methods used to achieve the result. The "individual" who proposed obtaining poison to put into the wells was only carrying a basic idea somewhat further than necessary, like Lt. Calley, who saw a quicker method of cleaning out the hamlet than rounding up the people and sending them "on their way."

No EVIDENCE WAS brought out in the trial to show foreknowledge on Medina's part of the true situation in the hamlet, and the story Pfc. Herbert Carter told two reporters has to be discounted, since he was unwilling to come forward and repeat it under oath: the night before My Lai, he claimed, he overheard Col. Barker and Capt. Medina talking; they had "found out there wasn't going to be no enemy there." In the trial, it was assumed that Medina did not make the discovery till the following morning—at a time the prosecution endeavored to place early and the defense, naturally, very late. But Eckhardt did not appear to see the importance of the point and slurred over it in his presentation, even though the facts elicited from Medina indicated extraordinary laxness for a commander who imagined he was in combat.

On landing, he set up his command post near the temporary LZ in the rice field and waited there while the first and second platoons began the sweep through the hamlet. As he explained, it was conventional to hold back the command group (together with elements of the third platoon, which was the destroy unit); if he had gone through in the first sweep, he might have been shot or captured by lurking VC or lost his RTO men —the lifeline to the TOC and the gunships. But he remained there stationary for *one and a half hours*. Though this was not brought out, presumably he could hear shooting and was able to distinguish the sound made by U.S. weapons from the sound made by Russian- or Chinese-supplied VC weapons. The village was reckoned to be about the length of three football fields and the width of one. Had there been 250 to 280 VC firing at Charlie Company and getting fire back, that would have made quite a lot of noise. Instead, he could have heard only U.S. rifles and machine guns turned on animals and villagers, *i.e.*, relative quiet. Yet he did not move till around 9 o'clock, when he made his brief sally of ninety yards into the hamlet and turned back on getting a radio message to go look for a VC with a weapon, off in the other direction, in the rice fields. This was the woman, lying on the dike, that he shot. She had no weapon and, as others testified, was already wounded.

Yet from his post in the rice field, at 8:30 A.M., an hour after touching down, he had issued a cease-fire to conserve ammunition. What made him do that? That was the gist of the question Col. Bobby Berryhill, the sleepy juror, sent up to the judge to give Medina: "When did you determine in your own mind that the action was uncontested?" Medina's answer was evasive. "Well, sir, throughout the morning there was indication that VC with weapons were fleeing, that they were being shot by the gunships, that they were being marked. [No real evidence was ever brought out of VC with weapons being shot. Hugh Thompson thought he saw one trying to run away. Col. Henderson claimed to have seen two bodies with weapons near My Lai 4 and to have marked the place with a smoke bomb. And there were the two or three he apprehended on the highway, descending in his chopper to make the capture, who turned out to be ARVN soldiers.] I had people going out. I didn't enter the village except for 75 meters and then I headed south. I started getting an awareness that something—that it was uncontested as far as the fact that the 48th VC Battalion wasn't there. We expected to have a big fight with them, and I just was not receiving the reports that would indicate that a battalion was in the village, and only that some VC with weapons fleeing had been killed. And this was somewhere between, I guess it went all the way up to close to 10 o'clock, sir; 9:30."

Col. Berryhill followed through with a second question, which the judge rephrased thus: "Did you normally give a stop firing or cease-fire order to conserve ammo in other operations if they were still contested?" The judge perceived what was behind this and hurriedly warned Col. Berryhill that he should not assume a position of advocacy. Col. Berryhill meant that you don't give a cease-fire order if you think the enemy is shooting at you; the cease-fire order, to save ammo, would date Medina's awareness at 8:30, and not at 9:30 or 10:00. But either Medina did not understand the second question as rephrased by the judge or understood it and dodged the implication in his answer by seeming not to get the drift.

Still, Col. Berryhill's point, even when duly appreciated, did not prove that Medina at 8:30 A.M. knew that his men were shooting women and babies. They might have been shooting pigs or water buffalo. But if he knew there were no enemy in the hamlet, why did he not proceed there, to check up on what was going on? His mistrust of Calley is in the record. Again he was evincing a morbid incuriosity. It is as if Capt. Medina desired to know as little as possible about this "combat assault," as if his main wish was to stay on the perimeter of it, while not actually running away.

One can well believe that he was innocent of the premeditated murder of not less than 100 persons, that indeed he took care to be innocent by refraining from investigation. Had he proceeded into the hamlet at 8:30 A.M., he would have been bound to apprise Major Calhoun at the TOC of what he found —no enemy and a whole raft of civilians—and initiated a query as to what to do about it. Do we go ahead and burn the hootches and blow up the brick houses and kill the animals and push all the people out of the village or what? But his job was to conduct a Search-and-Destroy mission. Why pass on information that would just throw a monkey wrench in the works? So he ordered the men to hurry. You could not count on Gen. Koster's reaction when the information reached him; in a moment of anger he might even rescind the OD.

By staying so long on the outskirts of the hamlet and out of the reach, apparently, of the TOC, Medina saved everybody a headache. When he entered, it was just about over: only a brick dwelling or two and the schoolhouse remained to be detonated, the hootches and rice stocks were burning, and there were some unavoidable dead, many more perhaps than he expected.

Assuming he stayed away out of circumspection, there remains a curious point to be explained. On landing, at 7:30, he radioed that the LZ was cold. But then, according to his testimony, he got a correction. "No. LZ hot. You are receiving fire." There is no real confirmation of such a transmission. As the judge noted, it is not heard on the tapes made by Capt. Lewellen. No independent witness, except Capt. Kotouc, a doubtful source, testified to hearing it or sending it. Medina could not give the code signal that would show where the message came from. Did he invent this phantom transmission to help account for not knowing, as he claimed, till 9:30 or 10:00 in the morning that the action was uncontested? Or did Col. Barker cut in sharply from the C-and-C ship to remind Medina that they *should* be receiving fire?

A final question arises. If the object was to wipe out the hamlet, why use infantry rather than air power? There could be a number of reasons. The Americal Division, which included Task Force Barker, was short of air power; Barker had to borrow some for the morning's assault. If B-52's were available, their usefulness was limited to area bombing, and there were "friendlies" operating in the region. Next, infantry is cheaper. Then morale. Charlie Company had been taking casualties without seeing any action—disturbing for the men—and this held, though to a lesser extent, for the whole division. Then, just at this time, a little more than a month after Têt and two weeks before Johnson's "abdication," the war had become very unpopular in the United States, and criticism, insofar as it was moral, centered on the bombing policy and the use of napalm. Finally, one of the aims must have been to develop intelligence (since there *were* VC units in the region), which meant taking prisoners. Medina was "developing intelligence" when he played William Tell with the detainee he was interrogating, who had been captured two days after the massacre. Bombers do not take prisoners.

In the event, using infantry was a fatal error. If the hamlet had been wiped out in an air strike, to the bombing crews it would have been just another mission, quickly forgotten. But face-to-face killing of non-combatants sticks in the memory of those who witness it. If civilians have to die, air and artillery

fire are felt by the military to be cleaner than point-blank shooting. Reluctance to believe in the men's savagery still persisted
at Fort McPherson, despite all the "exposure" given the facts
in the media. The judge and the jury foreman repeatedly
questioned witnesses in the evident wistful hope of assigning
large numbers of the corpses to the artillery prep and the gunships, as though bodies killed by those means somehow died
a natural death—true in a sense since random casualties from
machine-gun and artillery fire are a "natural" concomitant of
war.

Again and again that hope was dashed, and one could not
help sympathizing with the judge and Col. Proctor in their disappointment. Though it would have changed nothing for the
victims, most of us would prefer to think that those women and
babies and old men had died in a raid rather than been singled
out, one by one, for slaughter. Logic here is unpersuasive: the
deliberate individual killing of unresisting people *is* more re-
pugnant than the same result effected by mechanical means de-
ployed at a distance and without clear perception of who or
what is below. Even those who profess to see no distinction in
Vietnam between the crime of war and single acts of homicide
would be hard put to deny that distance does seem to count
in diminishing responsibility. Demonstrators shouting "Hey,
hey, LBJ, how many kids did you kill today?" were logically
right in viewing Johnson as the final cause, insofar as that could
be targeted in one person, but humanly they failed to convince,
since he was not the proximate cause and could not even be
said to have *intended* the slaughter of Vietnamese children in
the sense that Hitler intended the annihilation of the Jews in
the gas ovens.

WHATEVER LOGIC SAYS, remoteness from the scene attenuates responsibility unless a clear, almost telescopic intention can be shown. It is an old philosophic argument, which holds God innocent of the crimes of men; even though, to believers, He is the final cause of the scandal of existence, He does not exactly will it. The question greatly worried Dostoievsky, as well as a number of saints. But whether or not God is absolved, ordinary people have to absolve themselves of countless crimes committed with their complicity. You are eating a hearty meal, while somewhere a baby is starving. As the charitable appeals point out, you might have saved it. But pleading guilty to the charge does not give you license to strangle a neighbor's infant with your bare hands, as though to say "What's the difference? Both babies are dead, aren't they?"

If one and the same person can condemn Calley and still "live with" the B-52 raids in Laos and Cambodia, which he *knows* must be killing an unknown number of peasants on a daily basis, this only means that he is not totally callous. He knows if he stops to think, but mercifully he is not obliged to think twenty-four hours a day. There are knowledge and inescapable knowledge. Somewhere in between lies the toleration threshold, differing, obviously, in different people. In the air war, the magnitude of the effect produced by the mere everyday pressing of a button or releasing a catch surpasses the imagination of those concerned, which was not the case with Lt. Calley emptying and reloading his rifle or with the men who watched.

Pilots and bombardiers, unless they are captured, do not confront inescapably the murders they commit. Hence they are no more haunted by them, perhaps less, than the President of the United States and his civilian advisors, who sometimes wear a shamefaced or a brazen look. The airmen, like the generals, maybe because they are exercising a profession, are able to remain tolerant of themselves.

Medina's self-tolerance, in contrast to Calley, wriggling worm-like on a hook, was striking throughout his court-martial, which may account for the public disappointment in the trial as spectacle. In his testimony he told of "your old pucker factor going up" as the helicopters neared the LZ, with rocket ships and miniguns firing, but this seems to have been his unique moment of tension and pulsing excitement. On the ground, as the evidence showed, he had used considerable agility in keeping ugly sights and sounds at a distance and contrived to be as remote from the big carnage as somebody in an office building several miles away. When unavoidably he had to pass a body or a pile of bodies, he walked rapidly on, looking to neither the right nor the left, the way one skirts garbage in a big-city street. On the stand, except for technical know-how, he seemed no more "involved" in My Lai than a newspaper reader perusing a famine story from Biafra or Bangladesh. Unless you had seen his photos, you could not have picked him out in the courtroom as the defendant; leafing through the books of case material, he might have been one of his own lawyers.

To expect signs of repentance from a man in the dock is doubtless old-fashioned. Bluebeard, who killed 40 to 200 children, appeared at his trial dressed from crown to toe in white satin as a mark of contrition and expiation, even though, like Eichmann, he distinguished between divine justice and human justice and considered himself innocent before the law. In current America, where scarcely anybody believes in a higher law, to try a man for a crime is automatically to set up a defensive process, a hardening and stiffening of the new skin that closes off any entry for penitent thoughts, let alone egress for open admissions of guilt. Still, it was puzzling to see no traces whatever of the crime and its aftermath either in Medina, joking and whispering with counsel, or in the long file of witnesses from Charlie Company marching up to take the stand. It was as if they felt themselves to be permanently on trial and had assumed a defensive posture of unconcerned normality.

THEY HAD BEEN returned to life. Some were students and wore mod hair styles and counter-culture fashions. Others, being still in the service, could not display a sartorial cool but testified with a marked indifference, like transistors playing. Quite a few had become policemen and tended to rings and sideburns. One was in the anti-war movement; one was a pipe-fitter; one was an undertaker; one who had been a brassière salesman at the time of the Calley trial was now a carpet-installer.

Two, according to testimony, had killed young children: Oliver, the carpet-installer, by his own confession; Widmer, a student, who, incriminated by another witness, took the Fifth Amendment. Yet you would never think it to look at them, particularly Widmer, with a long stubborn meditative face, long light-brown hair and mustache, wearing a lavender shirt and red-and-white-striped tie; an occasional shifty dart of the eyes sidewise as he sat in the witness chair declining to answer made him seem less like a military killer than like a defiant hippie. From cheesy-faced Gene Oliver, guilt transpired, like sweat; yet his discomfort, one would have guessed, was caused

38

by the fear of being caught in a lie, rather than by any sense of shame for the act he was finally avowing.

If this fat inactive-looking man, a sharp dresser in a three-piece suit, cowboy boots, and ruby stickpin, was not wholly im-plausible as a war criminal, it was hard to take his word for it, even under oath. A surprise witness, he swore that it was he who had killed the child whose murder Medina was charged with ("Stop him, stop him, get him," etc.). During previous interrogations, Oliver had been mum on the slaying; in fact the whole account of himself he had given at the Calley trial had undergone radical revision. *Then* he said he had spent one and a half to two hours in the hamlet; *now* it was five minutes. According to his story now, he had killed the running boy on his own initiative, because he was aware of a sudden movement; he had never heard any order from Medina to shoot and of course he did not bother to "check it out," *i.e.*, to establish whether the child was actually dead.

When asked why he had not told the story earlier, he said, "It was something I had to bury"; what made him come forward, finally, was hearing that Medina was charged with premedi-tated murder on this count. So it was his conscience that drove him to speak, to save somebody he knew to be innocent. Yet he did not act like a person who has had a weight lifted from his spirit. He was highly ill at ease on the stand, now staring de-fiantly forward like someone who does not expect to be believed, now making a bizarre nervous grimace resembling a half-suppressed belch. During the recess following his testimony, he refused point-blank to be interviewed by the prosecution about his unexpected confession. Several days later, Eckhardt put him back on the stand, to accuse him of telling another witness (a

lie-detector expert) that he intended to kill him and Capt. Wurtzel: "I ask you under oath if you ever expressed a desire to
kill me?" Oliver denied it.

There was something very strange certainly and seemingly
unbalanced about Oliver. At the Calley trial, he had amazed
everybody by maintaining—the only witness ever to do so—that
there had been VC fire at My Lai 4: ". . . three AK-47 rounds
whistled over my head." But his confession here at Fort Mc-
Pherson could not be so lightly discounted. It was backed up by
another veteran—a Mormon, Michael Terry, also of the third
platoon, a neat student with sideburns and mustache, in a navy-
blue blazer. He heard a shot, he said, and twenty-five meters
away a young boy fell. It was Oliver, five meters off, who had
fired. Then Capt. Medina called out something that Terry's
religious scruples would not permit him to repeat. Under urging, he paraphrased: "Blankety blank, cease fire." As Oliver
told it, what Medina yelled was "It's only a kid," then "God
damn it, cease fire." Terry's careful spatial recollection, his
quiet manner, and scruple about the Second Commandment
made him seem an unusually trustworthy witness, with a clear
painstaking memory. Yet on May 1, 1969, as cross-examination
established, he had had the following exchange with Col. Wil-
son, a CID investigator: "Did you see any direct killing on the
ground?" "I don't remember. If I did, it didn't stick in my
memory." He now said his memory had been refreshed by
Gene Oliver.

Many of the witnesses, but especially those for the defense,
had told different stories when questioned earlier. Had they
changed, along with their testimony? There was Robert Lee,
who led off for the defense; he had been a medic in the first

(Calley's) platoon but had stayed to the rear with Sgt. Cowen. He had seen a few dead bodies that appeared to have been killed by rifle fire but no actual shooting by troops and had had no awareness that groups of defenseless people were being mowed down. By leading off with this witness, who did not meet Medina himself until evening, the defense was trying to show that it was possible for somebody (as Medina was claiming of himself) to spend the whole morning near and in the hamlet without any awareness of a massacre. Very good. But on September 17, 1969 this same witness had told an investigator that "women and children were being massacred, and I wanted no part of it. . . . I realized when I came into the village what was happening." On the subject of when and if he had heard a cease-fire order given, his testimony had also varied: in Oshkosh, Wisconsin, his home, he had told one story to the CID man and another to Capt. Wurtzel. To explain the discrepancies in his statements, he declared that the CID man had interrogated him without respite from around 2:00 P.M. till 11:00 at night; he had not been allowed to call his wife or take a break to eat—"I felt this man was putting words in my mouth." This last may have been true, but the record showed his statement had been taken at 4:40 P.M. When he had been interviewed by the prosecution, he said, in June, 1971, Capt. Wurtzel, instead of writing down his words, had just typed out a statement and given it to him to sign. But Wurtzel got up to state that there had been no typewriter in the examining room that day.

Lee's and Oliver's were among a number of cases where the government had failed to keep pace with the changing testimony of the witnesses and thus was caught flatfooted. The defense was better keyed in to Charlie Company's shifts of mood. But how can these be accounted for? It is true that people tend to tell an interrogator, particularly perhaps if he is an officer, what they think the interrogator wants to hear. It is also true that memory can be refreshed or, on the contrary, get hazy. Or one may think one has heard a figure pronounced ("The number 300 sticks in my head") but realize that one may have read it in a magazine. Yet the lapses and divagations of memory at Fort McPherson seemed to call for some special explanation. Among the prosecution's witnesses, there was not just confusion but monosyllabic obstinacy, hedging, backing off, refusal to state what the prosecutor was evidently counting on hearing, which suggested that a decision to clam up on or alter earlier testimony had been adopted not just by individuals but by a whole group. This may have been arrived at by joint consultation or through a sort of contagion from ideas and attitudes in the air.

WHEN THE MY LAI STORY first broke, there was general shock and horror. World headlines, editorials. Ron Ridenhour's long-ignored letter made him a hero. The Haeberle pictures appeared in *Life*. This created an atmosphere favorable to voluntary confession. Paul Meadlo went on television to avow what he had done. Other servicemen having no connection with Charlie Company confessed to war crimes *they* had committed. In this wave of repentance and belated truth-telling, fantasy no doubt entered, as always. Some men confessed, if not to imaginary crimes, to a greater criminal knowledge and complicity than they may actually have had. Others told of hearing conversations and witnessing incidents that may never have taken place: the angry officer with the clipboard, now descending from a helicopter, now at LZ Dottie giving another officer hell; the Shakespearean night scene of Col. Barker and Medina conspiring in a field tent or trailer and overheard by Pfc. Carter. In such an atmosphere, it is conceivable that a witness like Robert Lee, when talking to the CID, exaggerated his personal awareness of murder in the hamlet; wishing to feel *included*, he may have put words in his *own* mouth. The same with others who were talking eagerly to journalists.

After the Calley verdict, the wave of national remorse rapidly abated or took the new form of remorse for the conviction of Calley. Some of the men who had testified against him doubtless repented having talked, even if what they had said had been true. As the weird scapegoat theory gained currency (a scapegoat, to be one, must be innocent and expiating the crimes of others), hostility to the Army as the *real* criminal mounted. The infantrymen who had "finked" in the Calley trial probably said to themselves that, if they had it to do over, they would be less co-operative with the brass. Their second chance came. Called to testify against Calley's captain, they balked, changed their stories, could not remember, were not sure. Lee Bailey, outlining the defense case, gave an index of the new mood when he spoke in a sarcastic tone of "these so-called atrocities." Did he mean that My Lai did not happen or that it was not an atrocity? His remark drew no objection from Major Eckhardt, no reprimand from the judge; it just slid by, seemingly unnoticed even by newsmen.

Second thoughts came slowly to Policeman Louis Martin, a former radioman with the command group, who had given damaging testimony against Medina, which was weakened, though, by an unsavory past ("juvenile offenses") and by a story about a promotion refused him by Medina. He was a flashy nervous type, wearing a mustache and a yellow tie, who kept moving his tongue in his cheek as he testified, seemingly in quest of some bulky food deposit. He described a group of eight to twelve women and children in a "patio-type area," being guarded by some soldiers when the command group entered the hamlet; as soon as the command group passed, he saw them mowed down. Capt. Medina, he estimated, was ninety feet away. Shortly after giving this testimony, during a court recess, he went to the defense and confessed that he now "thought" it had been "inaccurate and misleading." Begging not to be put back on the stand, he agreed to take a lie-detector test because he "wouldn't like to see anybody get into trouble." He told the polygraph expert, who then testified for the defense, that the group of eight to twelve people he saw shot had possibly never existed: all his life, he revealed, he had had problems with "illusions and delusions."

Quite different was what happened to Michael Bernhardt, billed as the star witness for the prosecution. His record at My Lai 4 was clean: he had kept his rifle pointed at the ground, refusing to take any part in the slaughter. He was a middle-class boy of good appearance, attractive to journalists, to whom he had talked at length even before the Calley trial, and a friend of Ron Ridenhour. Medina had evidently been wary of him, as a youth with ethical hang-ups, way back in the Vietnamese graveyard where the company spent the night. In his letters, Ridenhour quoted "Bernie": " '. . . that evening Medina came up to me and told me not to do anything stupid like write my congressman,' about what happened that day." To the author of one of the Calley books, he described himself as a lifelong Republican with "absolute faith" in his government. With these credentials, he was bound to be listened to and he was said to be not only eager to testify but ready to come down hard on Medina, whom he considered directly responsible for the massacre. When he was announced, finally, on August 25, for the afternoon session, the courtroom was full of anticipation. Pressmen were guessing that he might have something to reveal today that had not been brought out in the Calley trial, and hopes, naturally, ran high.

But he had hardly taken the oath when Bailey was on his feet, demanding that the jury be sent out while the defense brought evidence to challenge his right to be heard. The jury went out, and under Bailey's questioning the stunned young witness wilted. The night before, he had had a conversation with Capt. Kadish; now he sat listening, incredulous, as his words were read back to him: "Didn't you say 'What I know about My Lai 4 is my business'?" "Didn't you tell Capt. Kadish that you had knowingly withheld evidence in connection with Article 32?" The pale fox-faced young man seemed to stagger in his seat. He must have believed that his talk with Kadish was private. Something apparently had given him the assurance that Kadish would not or could not take notes. Or he had been drinking, like the black witness, Spec-4 Heming, when Kadish collared *him*. Or on an LSD trip. Could Kadish have stood him a few companionable beers in some off-post roadhouse? Whatever the circumstances, Bernhardt's part in the night's conversation (Kadish's part was not divulged) sounds more as if he had thought he was "rapping" in some counter-culture bull session than being interviewed by an adversary lawyer. What emerged was simple and enormous: the lifelong Republican had turned against established authority.

" 'I have the prerogative as an individual of telling the truth or not.' 'I don't know whether I'll tell all the truth or not tomorrow.' 'I could lie or conceal the truth for a principle of justice.' 'What I *think* it is [the truth] is what is important.' 'I could tell an untruth to preserve not a person but a principle —namely justice.' " Did he remember Kadish asking him "Are you going to exercise that prerogative [of lying] tomorrow?" Hadn't he answered "Be surprised"?

Bernhardt jibbed at some of the wording and sometimes he opened his mouth as if to protest or explain. But the law was too fast for him. He never got a chance to tell what he had really meant, amplify, restore his statements to context, relate (what was evident from his reaction) how Kadish had conned him. He had the alternative of affirming or denying, and the fact that, for the most part, he was unable to deny showed him, alas, to be the opposite of what he had been boastfully claiming, in short to be a person wholly unskilled at lying.

What he had aired the night before were simply "movement" clichés, but to a military court unfamiliar with the language they were devastating. More in horror than in pity, the judge frowned down from the bench at the stricken witness. One of the guards, a young M.P. first lieutenant, shook his dark cropped head in wonder. He had done his basic training under Bernhardt, then a sergeant: "He was such a very gung-ho guy," he told a reporter.

Bailey moved on to anti-war activities. Kadish: "What are you going to tell the jury tomorrow if you are asked if you've taken part in anti-war demonstrations?" Bernhardt: "You'll get no. I've been to meetings." Kadish: "Is this a subversive group?" Bernhardt: "I'll take the Fifth on that." Now Bailey stopped reading and shouted in his own person: "Are your ideas of truth connected with a subversive group?" Bernhardt's "No" could hardly be heard. All the militancy had gone out of him. As Kadish's betrayal was borne in on him, he looked more and more disbelieving, as if he could not credit his senses. Nor could he expect understanding from Major Eckhardt. A short recess was declared, following which the prosecutor, cold and angry, rose: "We wish to withdraw the witness." Bernhardt, with a bitter look, climbed down from the stand and walked out of the courtroom, making, as he went, a finger gesture some called obscene in the direction of Kadish and Medina.

Another prosecutor might have fought for his witness. He might have drawn him out about the "principle" that would justify lying. Had Bernhardt really said that he would feel justified in lying to *this* court or to some hypothetical court, say, a Nazi one? Nobody at Fort Mac would doubt that a World War II soldier or resistance fighter had the right to withhold information by lying or other means from his Gestapo captors. The shock and astonishment in Bernhardt's face as he heard his statements read back suggested that he had made them in some utterly different connection. It was easy to imagine Kadish, playing on his "movement" vanity, leading him on to "rap" about imaginary eventualities: what would Bernhardt's attitude to the truth be if America became Amerika? If an attempt is made to reconstruct Kadish's side of the dialogue, Bernhardt's statements appear to fall into two categories. First, defensive maneuvers to elude Kadish's efforts to find out what he was

47

going to testify tomorrow: "Be surprised." Second, mere rambling generalizations of the vague argumentative kind that young people are prone to, regardless of their political orientation, so long as they picture themselves as somehow nonconformists.

Nothing in Bernhardt's conduct would appear to place him very far to the left. Indeed, had he been a far-out leftist, he would have been bound to take the position that he had nothing to say to a "bourgeois" court. But there he was, willing and eager to testify. The "subversive group," which the defense avoided naming, was probably something more like the Veterans against the War in Vietnam or the Mobilization than like the Weathermen or the PRP.

But if a case could have been argued for him, Major Eckhardt, Turk's-head pipe grimly clamped in his lantern jaw, was not the man to argue it. He dismissed his witness and lost the hope, if he had ever had one, of obtaining a conviction. Whatever Bernhardt might have testified remains unknown.

"I GET THE FEELING somebody is betraying Eckhardt," a young reporter whispered. He could not guess who. "Sloppy staff work" was the explanation generally offered when the prosecution was booby-trapped. It seemed as though they did not trouble to interview their own witnesses before putting them on the stand. Since Eckhardt and Wurtzel had their backs to the spectators' section during the awful undoing of Bernhardt, it was impossible to read their reactions. And had they known that that same bewitched night their witness Heming had been somehow persuaded to converse with Capt. Kadish after drinking four quarts of wine? Were they taken aback when he turned up in court late, hung over, and wearing a dashiki, which somebody might almost suspect had been supplied by the defense? Perhaps there was no way of controlling that irrepressible witness or monitoring his testimony, so that he would not mix up a major's oak leaf with a colonel's eagle. Yet the prosecution needed him badly; he was one of the few who would swear to seeing civilians shot in Medina's presence—a little boy, probably the one Widmer was accused of shooting, and a woman running through a paddy field.

It was the government's key witnesses—Heming, Bernhardt, Martin—that the defense was able to "get to," outside the courtroom, in private talks. The prosecution never "got to" a defense witness; there were no surprises or reversals on that side. Perhaps there were personality problems. Major Eckhardt gave the impression of being out of sympathy with the men he called on to testify, who were often bearded, long-haired, uncouthly dressed, a procession of drop-outs, whereas Bailey's witnesses all looked as if they had been counseled on "grooming" and the choice of suit and tie.

The reporter who felt Eckhardt was being betrayed had learned that the next witness, Frederick Widmer, had been telling the defense lawyers that he would not give the testimony the government was counting on from him. Maybe Widmer merely meant that he was going to take the Fifth Amendment. It happened one-two-three; in the course of a single day the government's prize exhibits went down like pins in a bowling alley. As soon as Bernhardt was dismissed, Widmer, cigarettes and sunglasses in his breast pocket, was seated in the chair. "I respectfully decline to answer, on grounds of self-incrimination." He was accompanied by counsel, Capt. Gary Myers, a young very handsome blond lawyer serving with JAG who had been assigned to represent him during the Peers Committee hearings and was still by his side now, having flown in from Washington with the Judge Advocate General's permission.

It was a dramatic turnabout. A Pentagon lawyer co-operating with the defense in blocking the testimony of a crucial government witness. Furthermore, what was at stake was a civil-liberties issue. In order to secure his testimony against Capt. Medina, the government was granting Widmer immunity from prosecution for anything he might say in the trial that could tend to incriminate him, *i.e.*, were he to be asked about the child the witness John Smail said he saw him shoot. Capt. Myers, backed up by Bailey, argued that this did not give him sufficient protection in his constitutional rights. Widmer would need not just testimonial but also transactional immunity, to cover the whole My Lai 4 transaction insofar as it affected him.

The government declined to grant transactional immunity, claiming it was unnecessary, and, after listening to arguments, the judge ordered Widmer to testify. When he still refused, the judge cited him for contempt, and the case was sent to federal court, with the Atlanta Civil Liberties Union—strange bed-fellow for the Pentagon—joining Capt. Myers in representing Widmer. The judge of the federal court decided in Widmer's favor.

Again, it was impossible to guess whether Eckhardt was prepared for these startling developments or whether they caught him off guard. It seemed clear, from the minute Widmer strode to the witness chair, that he was utterly determined not to testify. But was this because he really feared prosecution (he did not have much to worry about, judging by preceding acquittals, and besides he was out of the Army) or did his stubbornness on the point have some more interesting motive?

As with Michael Bernhardt, the public never knew. In contrast to Fort Benning, security was tight at the Fort McPherson courthouse. As witnesses stood down, Judge Howard carefully cautioned them not to discuss their testimony with outsiders. As far as the press was concerned, the warning seems to have been 100 per cent effective. Counsel for both sides also remained distant with reporters, like the defendant and his wife—no social mingling—as though a quarantine had been decreed. Lee Bailey's only "leaks" were made to mikes and cameras.

In the absence of any indiscretions, it is hard not to relate Widmer's unbudging posture to the post-Calley reaction, that is, to the "scapegoat" outcry. He was not going to be pushed around by authority, and the discovery of his constitutional rights became a rock he clung to, with Bailey's strong endorsement. But who in this instance was authority? Did not the judging and punishing arm in some sense represent the people, as against Medina and those high-ranking military witnesses who would swear that he was a strong commander, a forceful leader, a *professional* soldier"?

Widmer's determination, in any case, was matched by that of his defender, who appeared in the courtroom like some uncompromising puritan angel, wearing full regulation uniform that stood out dark and trim against the summer tans of military counsel and the M.P.'s on guard. Gary Myers was the Aubrey Daniel of the Medina case. One could imagine him as belonging to that idealistic cell of young lawyers in JAG who had argued for a Nuremberg-style war-crimes trial. That night he was at the Civil Liberties Union headquarters in Atlanta, where Charles

51

Morgan, the director, was giving a little press party for Lt. Col. Anthony Herbert, the insubordinate war critic, another Fort Mac client of the ACLU.

ALL THE DRAMA of the Medina trial had been compressed in the single day of August 25, before the Labor Day recess. But it was Calley's appearance, on September 13, that brought out the crowds. That morning, for the first time, tall curly-haired Major Russell, the doctor-artist, had a disappointment. In the drawing he failed to get the little green courtroom pass; too many regular pressmen were on hand. A correspondent even dropped by from the Washington *Post* (which up to then had been content with a stringer), taking the day off from Fort Meade. In the Press Center, waiting for the drawing, were adolescent girls and boys with long fair hair—not just the usual kids and large middle-aged women, like the redhead who turned up most mornings in a robin's-egg-blue textured stretch pants suit, a triple pearl choker and big pearl clip-earrings. It was like a reunion, that morning, for the reporters who had covered the Calley trial and, above all, for the network and wire-service cameramen who had been standing so long on their platform outside the courthouse with so little work to show for it. At last a front-page face. They were waiting with cameras trained as Calley came up the sidewalk, accompanied by his old-time lawyer, George Latimer: "Hi, Rusty." He made a jaunty awkward sign with his right arm, like "Be seeing you on the campus," and that was it. Once in the courthouse, he was not put on the stand. Through his lawyer, he took the Fifth, was seen to shake Medina's hand in the witness room, and was whisked away, back to Fort Benning. The Washington *Post* went back to the Henderson trial.

BAILEY'S ANNOUNCED PURPOSE in convoking Calley was to confront him with testimony from a new witness, Capt. Hicks. One day back in Vietnam, as Hicks's account would go, the two were exchanging war stories; Calley had described the My Lai incident and told him that Medina was "surprised" by the massacre. Since his defense at his own trial had been that he was acting on Medina's orders, it was natural that, faced with this new evidence, he would plead the Fifth, especially since his case was still on appeal. Bailey fully expected it. Calling him as a witness was a way of laying the ground for introducing Hicks's testimony, which the judge was likely to rule out as hearsay. In fact the judge did so rule but then reversed himself. To bring Calley to court and grandly permit him to go away silent ("There's no need to parade him here": Bailey) was skillful psychological pressure exercised on the judge to relax his view of the hearsay rule.

Calley's narative, *if* he told it to Hicks and *if* it was true, throws a few rays of new light on what happened in My Lai 4 that morning. In Bailey's summary, the massacre was "triggered" by the villagers' reaction to seeing their water buffalo shot. They cheered when the platoon came in (some newsmen understood "jeered"); then the point man shot a water buffalo, and they were quiet. After that, the angry men "opened up." In other words, if the population had continued to cheer, they would not have got killed.

The whole story is a bit perplexing, not least on account of

the cheer/jeer confusion. Assuming that My Lai 4 was a VC
hamlet (all "Pinkville" was VC territory), it is not likely that
the inhabitants would have cheered at the sight of the platoon.
Nor would they have jeered necessarily. A sullen silence was
the usual reception in such areas. But if the massacre somehow
grew out of the wanton killing of the livestock, the troops' behavior becomes minimally understandable. Under their company commander's direct order, they were committing a wicked
action, which some might have felt some premonitions of guilt
about if their consciences had not been assuaged by the promise
that there would be no civilians present. But it was one thing to
shoot up the animals, burn the rice stocks, and contaminate the
wells in the guaranteed absence of the population, and another
to have to do it with the people looking on. The sense of guilt
could then turn the guns on the silent watching people. Thus
the arch-responsibility goes back to the Medina and Barker
briefings, which ordered the cold-blooded annihilation of a
village.

At the same time, the question of calling Calley as a witness
pointed to a judicial weakness at the heart of the Medina proceedings. In the Medina trial, Calley could be called only as
a defense witness, and his answers, were they to exculpate
Medina, would incriminate Calley himself further, besides
making him liable to a fresh charge—perjury. He could not
be called by the government because the choice between his
credibility and Medina's had already been made at Fort Benning, when Medina was put on the stand to state that he had
given no orders for the killing of civilians. Calley's main defense, that he was acting under orders, was destroyed there by
Medina's testimony. The vote to convict Calley was a vote of

confidence in Medina's truthfulness and would be bound to play a role in any future trial Medina would face.

Aubrey Daniel anticipated this legal dilemma and elected not to call Medina as a witness for the prosecution. He evidently foresaw that this would hamper the government in trying Medina himself. It was the jury in the Calley case, over Daniel's objections, who demanded to hear Medina. Perhaps those non-legal brains did not understand the consequences for a future prosecutor of what they were doing. But the future prosecutors understood.

Before Medina's court-martial began, the government issued a significant statement: it did not propose to use evidence of what had been said in the defendant's pre-assault briefing in con-structing the case against him. *I.e.*, to prove the charge of premeditated murder, it could not rely on the evidence of the numerous witnesses who, in the Calley case and elsewhere, had sworn that the captain ordered them to kill "everything that breathed," "everything that moved," and so on. Government reliance on these witnesses would have retroactively confirmed Calley, whose lawyers might seize on the issue to demand a new trial for him. But without that evidence the government's case was handicapped to the point of being crippled. The prosecution admitted as much when on the eve of the trial it told reporters that the evidence against Medina was "skimpy."

True, though it was hardly the prosecution's place to pro-claim it. In fact quite a bit of "everything that breathed" testi-mony (also testimony to the contrary) did crop up, but the official case against him, in the murder of not less than 100 persons, rested on his mere awareness of the massacre, and awareness is very difficult to establish. If the government could have shown intent, awareness could be expected to ensue. That is, if I order you to kill everybody in the next room and then come in and find a pile of bodies, it will be hard for me to claim later that I "assumed" they had all committed suicide. But for a juror weighing the evidence in the Medina trial, intent had to follow awareness: no awareness, no intent. The powerlessness of the government to insist on the alleged criminal content of the orders reduced Medina's role at My Lai 4 to that of a chance spectator.

He did nothing to stop the killing until around 11:00 A.M., when he ordered or did not order a cease-fire (testimony on this was conflicting, to put it mildly), he gave no medical aid, he noticed a few dead bodies. Except when shooting the woman and ordering (or not ordering) the boy shot, he behaved like a casual passer-by, and who can prove what a passer-by saw, let alone what conclusions he drew or should have drawn?

It was not enough for the government to place Medina through eyewitness testimony in the vicinity of several killings. It had to be proved that he saw them, which he denied. For a witness to infer that Medina saw them or could have seen them was not proof. At best, it tended to show likelihood. But just here the fallibility of memory, especially in matters of arithmetic, cast doubts: how many meters, how long a time? Even the most affirmative prosecution witnesses could not do better than vaguely estimate distances, and the sum total of all that uncertainty gave the benefit of the doubt to the defendant, to the point where one felt the jury might wonder whether Medina was ever anywhere near the hamlet since nobody was sure of having seen him there at any fixed point of space or time.

The inability of government witnesses to "pinpoint" a given

action was used, naturally, by the defense to impeach their credibility: "How far were you from Capt. Medina? Was it eight feet, ten feet, a hundred yards?" "Was it less than an hour, more than an hour, less than a half hour, less than fifteen minutes? Speak up!" The peremptory fire of questions shook the men on the stand, who usually ended with a frightened "I don't remember," which caused Bailey to nod in satisfaction, as though such an admission nullified all their testimony.

In the military setting, imprecision seemed damnable, and nobody stopped to think that a witness who could crisply state that he was nine and a half meters from the defendant when an old man was pulled out of a hootch and that the time was eleven hours thirty-five minutes might be more of a fantasy artist than one like former Spec-4 Heming who disdained the yard-stick. "How near was Capt. Medina?" "How *near*? Why, he *standing* right *there* on the trail." As a witness, Heming had the refreshing habit of treating whatever he reported as self-evident, which indeed is how experience seems to everybody when still in its pure state. To common sense, "near" requires no further definition; it is the opposite of "far."

Yet even when such a confident witness could place Medina within sight or earshot of a killing, it only established his location. Consciousness is something else. How can anybody be sure that somebody standing next to him sees what he sees? Has the other turned his head away at the crucial moment, was his view blocked? Still less if the other is several yards ahead or behind. Suppose the effect is cumulative and reason says, "Well, if he missed seeing the old man shot, he must have seen the running woman" or "What about the noise, the M-16 and machine-gun fire, the screaming?" this still is not proof,

57

but speculation. If Medina was to be presumed innocent, the jury had to keep before its mind the possibility that he failed to see what others saw, since nobody *saw* him see it. As for noise, there were the helicopters overhead making a terrible racket.

It could happen that somebody would spend four hours in a small bamboo-shaded hamlet just missing a hundred-odd murders. The jury, bearing this in mind, seemed duty-bound on the basis of the evidence presented to find Medina innocent even if it guessed him to be guilty.

Yet he was not a simple spectator, but the company commander. On the basis of the defense evidence alone any jury could have convicted him of dereliction of duty with little or no debate. His absence from the scene, attested to by himself, and almost total lack of liaison with the green men under him would lay him open to the charge of cowardice, if he really believed the action to be contested. If, on the other hand, he knew almost from the start (as indicated by the cease-fire-to-conserve-ammo) that the action was uncontested, his conduct was delinquent to a bizarre degree, lacking even the excuse of battlefield panic. There was also his admission, already made at the Calley trial, that he took part in the later cover-up—more dereliction, since according to the code an officer was bound to report immediately any atrocities that came to his knowledge, and in addition to that, misprision of a felony, since he helped fudge the figures.

Why was he not tried for dereliction, misconduct, and misprision of a felony, as well as war crimes? The question was widely asked, especially after he checked in at the Henderson court-martial and freely testified to having lied to Henderson, the Peers Panel, and the Army Inspector General's office. When the press put the question earlier, during his own trial at Fort Mac, the prosecution's answer was that it was customary to drop the lesser charge in favor of the greater one. In fact, one count against him in the original indictment had been suppression of information and this was dropped when the additional charge was decided on. Even so—said some people who would have rather seen Medina in jail than waving an Honorable Discharge diploma at photographers—if the government felt the evidence on the war-crimes charge was "skimpy," why did it not stick with the lesser charge and obtain a conviction, instead of letting him slip out of the Army into Lee Bailey's helicopter plant?

THE IDEA THAT there was a conspiracy to let Medina get home free was sometimes hard to avoid at Fort Mac. To some observers of the trial, the fact that the judge and four out of five of the jurors were native-born Southerners was in itself a suspicious circumstance—almost proof that the government was working for an acquittal, whether or not Eckhardt and Wurtzel were parties to such an understanding or ignorant pawns. Southerners, it was argued, on account of their military traditions, would incline to sympathize with a career officer and see him as a victim of liberal hypocrisy. No My Lai 4 trial, it was pointed out, had taken place at a northern post, where attitudes might be expected to be a little different, even at the officer level. Why try a Montrose, Colorado, man in the Deep South for war crimes committed in Vietnam unless you want to give him a break?

But the preponderance of Southerners, though partly explained by the trial's venue (the Army tries to rotate officers and men back to where they came from, where they have homes and family ties), was not guaranteed by it. In the Calley trial, at nearby Fort Benning, the jury had been split fifty-fifty between Northerners and Southerners, and Judge Kennedy's home town was Spencer, Iowa. As for the venue, Medina had done his officer's training at Fort Benning, so that it was normal that he should be assigned there while awaiting trial. When his duty-station was later changed to Fort Mac, this was because of an administrative decision to group all the cases directly related to My Lai 4 at Third Army headquarters, in the interests of efficiency and to economize on the travel of counsel and witnesses, according to the Army's announcement. Cases indirectly related to My Lai 4, like that of Col. Henderson, were to be grouped at Fort Meade. It seems logical that the headquarters of the Third Army, covering the southeast of the U.S., should have been chosen, but why Calley's case was left at Fort Benning is not clear, unless preparations for it were already far advanced.

The southern cast of the judging body at Fort Mac is best excused by the southern cast of the Army itself. Southerners predominated among the troops in Vietnam, more so perhaps in other ranks and up to the colonel level than at the top. It was a war of crackers and rednecks (including officers), urban blacks, *chicanos* like Medina, poor Italians, Poles, Puerto Ricans. As the biggest under-privileged minority, the South naturally sent the most boys. Charlie Company, testifying in all the black and white varieties of southern speech, was an aural demonstration of that. So it did not seem inappropriate that Prosecutor Eckhardt should be an Ole Miss graduate, that Capt. John Truman should be from Independence, Missouri, that the M.P.'s should be southern and soft-spoken, that even Major Russell, with his drawing-board, should be a Virginian, that most of the newsmen and the two pretty newsgirls, one blonde and one brunette, should be southern too.

It was an easygoing Deep South show, featuring southern hospitality: Judge Howard repeatedly leaning forward (without being asked) to fill Medina's Coke glass with water as he gave his testimony. The South melted into the Army: Col. Bobby Berryhill's name brought back a bevy of colonels in South Vietnam: Col. Derryberry, Col. Culpepper. . . . And like the Army in Vietnam, and to the same degree, Atlanta, downtown, was integrated, on the job level, in motels, hotels, and restaurants. As the site of an earlier war crime—Sherman's march, which had burned the city to the ground—and the birthplace of Coca-Cola, it made a suitable background. No ante-bellum houses, no history-haunted monuments, nothing to see but a Disneyish reconstruction of the Civil War called the Cyclorama and a sunken maze of souvenir shops and Gay Nineties or frontier-type steak houses called the Underground, a tall hollow-centered de-luxe hotel resembling a maximum-security prison, and a "contemporary" FBI building. Downtown Atlanta did not look as if anybody lived there: they just held salesmen's conventions all year round. Somebody indigenous had resumed General Sherman's work and razed the center of the city to construct parking lots, multi-level garages, motels with swimming pools and free ice-dispensers in a simple cadre of insurance-company skyscrapers: Clear and Hold.

So the jury was not rigged, and Judge Howard in his little flowing black tie was a good man and as free from bias as any prosecutor could hope for. There was no conspiracy to hold the trial at Fort Mac rather than Fort Dix or Fort Lewis, Washington. It had just worked out that way, and the outcome would probably have been the same wherever the trial was held. The American public as a whole seemed quite content with Medina's acquittal (of all the telephone calls received at the Press Center following the verdict only one protested) while at the same time feeling cheated by it. Those who cursed the Army for convicting Calley now sneered at the Army for letting Medina off. Though with less assurance, for the fact is that it was public opinion and not the jury that decided. Leaving out the part played by President Nixon in reducing the Calley conviction and the part played by Wallace and the extreme right in heating mass fury, the determination of the left not to consider *anybody* a war criminal short of a three-star general has meant that no three-star general will ever sit on the accused bench. Medina was a transition figure between the war-makers and the "animals" (as the airmen in Vietnam called the infantry), and his acquittal halted a process that might have gone up the ladder of responsibility. If Medina had been in jail, it would have been harder to acquit Col. Henderson. With Henderson in jail . . . The finger would have steadily pointed upward. Had public pressure been maintained, it might not have been left to the Army to decide when enough was enough. If there was a conspiracy, it was a great nationwide breathing together of left, right, and much of the middle to frustrate punishment of the guilty.

STILL, WAS MEDINA *legally* guilty of anything worse than criminal dereliction that day? On the additional charge, after the defections of Heming, Bernhardt, Widmer, and Policeman Louis Martin (each in his own fashion, they let the side down), the government was left with the depositions of Minh and Phu, and the testimony of former radioman Kinch, now a private detective, who was sure he heard the captain say: "That's enough shooting for the day. The party's over." The sole witness, though, who remembered anything similar ("'It's over. The firing's over.' Or something like that") tended to weaken confidence in the accuracy of Kinch's memory rather than corroborate him. Other government witnesses could merely place Medina "in the area" of the killings, and Smail, a former rifleman, who said Medina was close by when Widmer shot the child, added that the captain had "his head down" when it happened.

Besides the eyewitnesses, there was the testimony of the polygraph expert Brisentine, who said Medina told him that between 9:30 and 10:30 he felt he had lost control of his men. If it was as early as 9:30 and Medina was then where he said he was (outside the hamlet), the question arises, how did he know? And if by some undetermined means he knew, why didn't he do something? Or was he not where he said he was?

There were a few straws as well supplied by Nick Capezza, a New York City housing detective, formerly a medic, who kept pausing in his declarations to ruminate on a cud of gum. He remembered that when a report came in that a helicopter pilot had seen wild firing Medina got on the radio to Calley. "He asked Calley what the f—— was going on." "Had you ever heard Capt. Medina talk to Calley like that before?" "Usually in person, not on the radio." Calley, he said, then reported "about 30" civilians killed in cross fire. Like Heming, Capezza had seen a tall thin officer carrying a clipboard at the landing zone. In the detective's recollection, he was wearing a helmet.

Medina did not cite the "What the f——" transmission. On the first round, in direct examination, he said he had tried to reach Calley after seeing the group of bodies on the trail but had only got his RTO. Under cross-examination, he hedged. "I possibly may have called Lt. Calley and said 'What's going on up there? I just seen a bunch of bodies.'" This was at the time of the Carter medivac, between 10:30 and 11:00. According to Medina, the report from headquarters that a pilot had seen wild firing came later. "And what did you do when you heard that?" "I rogered the transmission and I radioed the platoon leaders to make sure that their people were not shooting indiscriminately and killing noncombatants, sir." It was important to Medina to place the transmission and hence his own first awareness as late as possible in the morning. The same with the cease-fire.

Testimony on all of this, including Medina's own, was extremely contradictory and confusing. Some heard a cease-fire given; some did not; and the estimated times for it varied widely. As for radio contact with Calley, Medina had two or more different recollections. Eckhardt: "Did you not tell Mr. Brisentine that you had no contact with Lt. Calley at all except for one time when you possibly issued a cease-fire after the boy was shot and when you did issue a cease-fire order after a radio communication from Major Calhoun?" "Yes, sir, I believe that's correct. To the best of my recollection that's what I think I told him." "You had not—is that accurate—you had no contact with Lt. Calley other than those two times?" "I could not recall at that time all the transmissions I had with those platoon leaders. I didn't make a log. . . ."

Yet under cross-examination he related in detail two other transmissions with Calley. One was between 7:30 and 9:30 A.M. "There was a report from Lt. Calley that a helicopter pilot had landed, and I asked him what's the matter. And he says 'He don't like the way my platoon—I am running my platoon.' And I says 'What did you tell him?' . . ." Again, somewhere between 8:00 and 8:30 (before or after the other message?), he received from Calley a KIA report of sixty-nine. Eckhardt: "Did you inquire of Lt. Calley whether these were combatants or noncombatants?" "No, sir. They were reported as VC, sir." "Did you inquire of Lt. Calley whether these 69 people were armed or not?" "I asked Lt. Calley to—how many weapons. And he said they were still checking." In all these recollections, he omitted any mention of the "about 30 civilian casualties from crossfire" answer that Capezza said had come from Calley. Possibly (sloppy staff work) Eckhardt had forgotten Capezza's testimony. He did not ask Medina about it during these exchanges, and the opportunity did not return.

THE CASE AGAINST Medina, such as it was, resided largely in the interstices of his own testimony, which was full, as they say, of holes, not necessarily incriminating but leaving room for further explanation. The feeling remained that the full story of My Lai 4 was still to be told, not the details of the massacre but what lay behind it. The strange conduct of Medina, which could not be hidden, was the only clue left lying in plain sight.

But the Army was not clearly interested in raising speculation but in doing its official duty, which was trying Medina. If he had not been tried, questions would have been asked.

Here perhaps lies the motive for the government's decision to attach the additional charge, so elusive of proof, to the bill of particulars against him, even if this involved dropping the lesser charge, easily provable, of misprision of a felony. As has been said, the additional charge, dated April 1, 1970, was a second thought on the part of the Army. One can see the substitution of an unprovable charge for a provable charge as part of a general whitewash, which would leave Medina free and the officer corps with one less convict in its ranks. But one can also see it less as a cunning maneuver to defeat justice than as a normal exercise in public relations.

Some PR-wise colonel in the Third Army command may well have had a brainstorm one morning: "Hey, if we don't try Medina on the big charge, people will ask why! Maybe we'd better stick it in. We won't get a conviction, but our image will look clean." "But, sir, if we do that, we ought to drop the misprision of a felony count. In law it's not customary to try a man for a felony and for misprision of it at the same time. If somebody commits a felony, naturally he endeavors to conceal it, sir." "OK, drop the misprision count. They've got Henderson on that anyway, over at Fort Meade."

Such PR thinking is a mere businesslike reflex in U.S. institutional life and carries no hint to the thinker that he is embarking on a deceitful plot. If challenged, he would reply that he was only working within the accepted system. To avoid raising questions in the public mind is seen as a laudable aim by

advertising-conditioned officials who believe in their product—
in this case, the U.S. Army.

In an institution like the Army, it is stupid to ask questions
and clever to anticipate any that may come from the outside.
Nothing could have illustrated that better than the contrast
between the helicopter crewmen and Capt. Medina, as brought
out at Fort McPherson. If there were American heroes at My
Lai, they were the bubble-ship pilot, Chief Warrant Officer
(now Capt.) Hugh Thompson, and his door gunner, Lawrence
Colburn. The two were later decorated—with a misleading
allusion to "cross fire"—for evacuating Vietnamese civilians
they saw cowering in a bunker. Thompson and his crew made
three rescue lifts, on their own, independently of any orders,
and with rifles on the ready to shoot any man of Charlie Company who tried to interfere. As Colburn had related it earlier,
Thompson "told us that if any of the Americans opened up on
the Vietnamese, we should open up on the Americans. . . . He
stood between our troops and the bunker. He was shielding the
troops with his body." The pilot of a gunship, Dan Millians,
and his co-pilot, Jerry Culverhouse, following on Thompson's
initiative, also helped in the rescue; they did two lifts.

It was what they had seen from the choppers that prompted
their intervention—approximately 150 dead civilians (Millians), fifty to seventy-five Vietnamese in the ditch who "looked
wounded," small children, and "I remember one fairly aged
male" (Culverhouse), headless babies (Thompson). What was
visible to them can hardly have been totally invisible to Barker
in his command-control ship, which Millians said he saw hovering just outside the village.

On Thompson's first landing, he tried to get medical assistance for the wounded. "There was some friendlies just east of the ditch. I motioned to one of them to go help the wounded." But nobody moved. The pilot had a slow sad reminiscent way of shaking his head, as though in sighing harmony with his negative answers. Bailey's tactics of harassment he seemed hardly to notice, brushing off the lawyer's sarcasms like an inconsequential swarm of midges. It was the same with the other helicopter crewmen, whose mildness and almost simple-minded sincerity resisted all Bailey's battery of insinuation—quirked eyebrows, outthrust dubious lower lip, sudden changes of pitch. While standing at the lectern, he had a habit, perhaps designed to be frightening, of wrapping his arms around himself like his own python. From one of the gunship pilots, the lawyer's efforts to shake his testimony elicited a big humorous smile. They had all seen pretty much the same things and gave their accounts with a sort of peaceable weariness, as if it would be nice to oblige the defense and remember something different.

It had begun with Thompson's hovering over the hamlet in his OH 23 observation craft. He noticed something peculiar— dead bodies all over the place. It made him wonder, so he circled and hovered some more. "I'd seen some things that at the time I couldn't understand why they'd happened." He shook his head, paused, and repeated in a bemused voice, *"I couldn't understand."* The bodies in the drainage ditch, "they were not resisting type people." As he circled, he started to reason: they might have been shot by gunships, but the Vietnamese, being used to air attacks, would not take shelter, he thought, in an open ditch. If they had been killed in a cross fire, the G.I.'s would have just left them where they fell, for their own people

68

to pick up later. It was funny the way they were stacked up like that.

Going back in his memory, under the prosecutor's prodding, Thompson kept twisting and pulling down his lower lip, in a lengthy act of reflection. He too was Georgian—from Decatur—blond, slightly adenoidal, slow of speech, and dogged, extremely ordinary, like his predecessor on the stand, Capt. Culverhouse, who resembled a small wood animal. In comparison with some of the sharpies of Charlie Company, the pilots seemed rural, almost retarded.

The uncomprehending Hugh Thompson flew lower, right above the rice crops, to clear up the questions in his mind. He "saw a woman laying on a dike and popped smoke on her" to signal for a medic. (The defense claimed the smoke signal was understood as "VC with weapon"—a message that eventually reached Capt. Medina.) She had a wound in her abdomen. Then "a captain walked right up to the woman." He nudged her with his foot and retracted, walked away, and fired his weapon. She died. Next the pilot landed where he had seen "a black individual with his weapon pointed into the ditch" with the people in it. He had his argument with Calley and took off with some wounded on the first of his rescue lifts. On the last he flew out a small child who looked wounded and was clinging to its dead mother. He took him to Quang Ngai Civilian Hospital. "My fuel was getting real low." At the TOC he reported the killing of civilians. He had already reported the wounded he had marked with smoke for the gunships to pick up.

The next witness, former Warrant Officer Larry Colburn, was now a student. His testimony was identical with the pilot's except in very small particulars. He said the woman on the dike had her eyes open. She moved them and looked up at the heli-crew. Then, after the smoke-dropping, Medina arrived with the command group. "He turned her over with his foot and shot her." He remembered, yes, that she had flinched. Thompson remembered it too. But neither could be certain whether she flinched after or before the captain shot her. Colburn was slightly more positive than Thompson that the flinch came after the shooting—a reflex movement—but he would not swear to it. He *thought* it was after, and neither Eckhardt nor Bailey could get him to improve on that.

The flinch, described by both crewmen as a twitch or shudder, became in Medina's testimony a sudden movement that caused him to think she was going to throw a grenade at him. That was not how the episode had looked from the air ("As I remember it, he turned her over with his foot and shot her. That was all," Colburn said over and over), but of course from the air they could not see into Medina's state of mind, and Bailey got Col-burn to admit that if he had been in the captain's place and had thought she had a grenade, he would probably have done the same thing.

Despite this triumph, the defense seemed irritated by the fact that it could not shake both witnesses' emphatic certainty that *first* the captain had turned the wounded woman over with his foot; this had preceded any twitch, flinch, or movement. Bailey and Kadish may have felt that this sequence, though it did not prove murder, put their client in an unflattering light. If somebody is visibly wounded (the bleeding could be seen from the air), is the first step in first aid to turn her over with your booted foot and start to walk away?

At every point, Medina's conduct, on seeing dead and

wounded persons, was diametrically opposite to the conduct of Thompson and Colburn. Yet unlike Medina, Thompson and Colburn had no military responsibility for the men at My Lai. They had no business landing in the middle of what was supposed to be a battle to conduct rescue operations of enemy civilians—still less to interfere with the way Calley and his men were handling the operation. And yet they did.

Larry Colburn testified gently and softly, with many pauses for thought. He seemed, if not unwilling to testify, unwilling to remember the scene once more. Under Eckhardt's questioning, he tended to answer in monosyllables. "You saw one boy alive in the ditch." "Yes." His voice was low, slightly hoarse. "Movement?" "Yes." "Blood?" "Yes." He had softish clean long hair and a long projecting jaw. When he was asked to describe the crewmen's efforts to extricate the live child from the heap of corpses, he volunteered with a sad half-smile: "Specialist Andreotta [the third crew member], he was covered with blood."

These mild gentle witnesses seemed to rub on the court's nerves. Eckhardt's co-ordination of questions to their answers was sometimes so awkward that the judge, impatient, took over the examination. And Judge Howard was testy with both of them, doubting the ability of their bubble ship to hover as low and as long as they said, skeptical about the height of the crop in the paddy field. Like Eckhardt, he kept forgetting Thompson's rank ("Mr.—I mean Captain—Thompson") and became openly derisive about the pilot's refusal to give precise distances. The position of the woman on the dike led to wrangles: Thompson remembered her lying on her side facing one way, and Colburn, he *thought*, facing the other but also on her back. The judge, fed up with Colburn, suddenly had a new idea: maybe

71

she had been standing on the dike. *"Standing?"* Colburn's voice was incredulous (had the judge forgotten the stomach wound?). Then quietly, *"Oh, no."* Here was an instance of the court's tendency to slip into a dreamy fugue in which everything in the My Lai massacre would turn out to have a natural, military-manual explanation: gunship strafing, artillery fire, a standing woman with a grenade. . . .

WHAT CAME OUT of Thompson's and Colburn's testimony was the inescapable truth of a massacre. More disturbing still, the fact that to a very ordinary intelligence (Thompson's), the sight of the bodies urgently raised questions that to an ordinary intelligence would seem to want serious answers. Thompson's density, his puzzled inability to *"understand,"* were a sort of saving slow-wittedness. The picture of him hovering in his helicopter trying to comprehend gave a simple measure by which to judge others, who from General Koster on down acted like the three wise monkeys: see no evil, hear no evil, speak no evil.

Unlike the disbelieving pilot, they knew the score in Vietnam. It could not puzzle them to find civilian corpses lying around: sometimes the boys got rough. A smart commander did not criticize every little thing. When Ernie Medina saw some bodies, he did not stupidly start *thinking*. He promptly attributed them to gunships or maybe artillery fire—a military response as automatic as a knee jerk and showing excellent co-ordination: if you see something wrong, blame it on some other service and keep going. So the Navy pilots on the U.S.S. *Enterprise*, when told of photographic evidence of bombing of civilian targets in North Vietnam, genially blamed the Army, and no doubt vice versa.

One might ask where Thompson and Colburn had been during their service in Vietnam that they were still able to be shocked by heaps of civilian dead. Did they suppose this was a clean war? Evidently yes, as was shown by Thompson's frantic indignation, his repeated appeals to higher authority to *do* something to stop the slaughter. His disbelief in what his eyes were showing him was companioned by a touching belief in the willingness of his superiors to correct what in his view *had* to be a ghastly mistake. Yet his faith in the officer corps (even though he had just observed captain's bars on the man taking aim at the woman), what others would call his simple-mindedness, again, were saving graces, as it has turned out. Had it not been for the pilots' complaints to Major Watke, which were in fact passed on, the Ridenhour letter, when it was at last sent by Congressman Mendel Rivers to the Army for investigation, would probably have got little attention. But because of Thompson and Colburn, the Army already knew there was corroboration.

Also Thompson was right in imagining he had seen something exceptional. Despite what Americans seem to like to think, the My Lai 4 massacre was different from the haphazard rapes and killings committed by the "animals," from some airmen's playful "gook hunting," and the regulation torture of prisoners practiced by officers and NCO's or, more often, watched by them without comment as the ARVN went on with the job. In fact, the only comparable big atrocity yet on record took place the same day, in the same locality, at the My Khe 4 sub-hamlet, where Bravo Company of Task Force Barker killed 90 to 100 civilians. This was the other salient of Operation Muscatine— Search and Destroy. The commotion caused by reports racing in to the GRVN village chief, for once in advance of VC denunciations, showed that these atrocities went far beyond the level of violence that had grown to be considered routine.

Thompson seems to have been a conventional southern boy with a conventional faith in the war. He was personally ready to wage it beyond the call of duty. That very morning, in his little bubble ship, he had already exceeded his orders—to scout for VC and report them to the gunships. Catching sight of a Vietnamese male running away from the hamlet whom he judged (by the weapon and the uniform) to be a Viet Cong, he pursued him, shot, and missed. This episode is very much to the point. Had Thompson and Colburn been opposed to the war, on moral or political grounds, their reaction and conduct would have had less value as a measure by which to judge the reactions and conduct of Medina. Nobody at that time would have expected a career officer in Vietnam to behave like a Quaker elder or an SDS militant; still, he was expected to conform minimally to the standards of his kind. In contrast to Thompson and Colburn (who was then only nineteen years old), Medina of course failed miserably, and it could be argued that the presence of the two in the courtroom was actually prejudicial to the defendant. That was perhaps why Judge Howard was so unhappy with them.

Yet if Medina's court-martial proved anything, it was that the standard of behavior exemplified by the pilots and crewmen was a dead letter. The Army code of justice under which the trial was being held had become an historical curiosity without anybody's taking official notice of the fact. How else could it happen that officers and former officers enlisted by the defense as *character witnesses*—e.g., Brig. Gen. Lipscomb, Col. Luper,

Col. Blackledge, Major Calhoun, Capt. Kotouc—had been under investigation for criminal irregularities in connection with My Lai and, in two cases, actually been charged? The god-given thickness of Thompson was not to be aware of this evolution in Army morals. He was culturally retarded, maybe because of a rustic background, which had not kept him abreast of changes in civilian morality while he was growing up—for of course the Army was not evolving in a vacuum. Far from being sealed off from society, the U.S. Army is porous, and those who leave it are readily absorbed into the social tissue. If the career preference of the men of Charlie Company, on getting out of the service, was evidently "policeman" or "detective," that of the retired-officer character witnesses was "salesman." And Medina was praised not just for his professionalism but for his "warmth" of personality—a consumer criterion now widely accepted by Americans (including the counter-culture) as some sort of ethical evaluator. Only a conflict of scheduling spared the court Col. Henderson as a witness to Medina's outstanding character.

DURING THE TRIAL, the men on the stand suffered much harassment for their inability to quote exactly what Medina had said. "Or words to that effect" was the saving formula on which most fell back. An inadequacy with words, shown by nearly everybody connected with the proceedings, came to seem intrinsic to the mentality behind My Lai. Not just bad grammar—"I seen," "She was laying"—which was so common in the mouths of both officers and other ranks that it got to be courthouse standard English. Even F. Lee Bailey, who had some pride of rhetoric, talked about the "woman laying," with a wonderful air of

75

noblesse oblige. But the failure of universal education (more than half of the men of Charlie Company were high-school graduates or better) evidenced by simple bad grammar was less depressing than the monotonous and often ignorant use of "educated" phraseology, *e.g.*, the word "infer" taken to mean "imply" or just "indicate": "He inferred to me that we should keep quiet." The worst language-murderers were the lie-detector experts, Brisentine and Harelson ("Medina may have inferred to his men to kill everyone in the village"), who were also fond of the word "transpire" to mean "happen," of such expressions as "Artillery would be placed into the village" (*i.e.*, "would fire on the village"), and of redundant prepositions ("Capt. Medina described to me as to how she was laying").

Brisentine, dark, "keen-eyed," with bristly short gray hair and an incisive widow's peak, wearing a dark-brown suit, well accessorized, and heavy dark-brown horn-rimmed glasses, was obviously anxious to present himself as an educated, eagle-like intellect—a synthesis of confessor and mind surgeon. His words and phrases seemed to have been born in a briefcase, like the compendious one he carried. Instead of "then," he invariably said "at that time"; instead of "before," "prior to," instead of "about," "regarding." The combination of this business-letter diction with unerring faults of grammar made his testimony sometimes so obscure that you had to divine what he meant, as though he were an oracle. This may have been part of the intention.

Harelson was a Middle Westerner with sideburns, dressed in a dark-green suit, who had spent twenty-one years in what he called "the polygraph business." It was he who had extracted Louis Martin's confession to having illusions and delusions. He seemed less concerned than Brisentine with making the razor-sharp impression of a successful prober of souls and came on as a sort of neighborhood practitioner occasionally called in by the cops. Now and then he forgot to say "regarding" and used the simple "about." It sounded as if he had once taken a correspondence course in home psychiatry: "I asked him about his youth background." One reason the trial was boring was that so many of the participants were verbose, boring people.

It was natural, though, that "experts" close to the apparatus of government and police work should talk in an administrative jargon as remote from human speech as possible. What was sadder was to hear this jargon from the infantrymen of Charlie Company: "a patio-type area," "the initial insertion," always "in the area," never "around there" or "in that part of the hamlet." And "an individual" or "the individual," meaning usually a person that the witness does not care to identify more precisely but also, preceded by an adjective, meaning somebody praiseworthy, as in "a very fine individual."

Men who had formed the habit of speaking like a letter from a credit company or a summons to appear in court were oblivious of their remoteness from normal communication. During the reading of the Minh and Phu depositions, it was clear that Eckhardt was not always getting through to the two interpreters. He did not suspect that if he had once said "before" instead of "prior to," they might have had less trouble in understanding his questions. It was Eckhardt, rather than they, who could not speak simple English. Similarly with bald Capt. Kotouc, the company intelligence officer, who had large glazed blue eyes, large protruding ears, and a small protruding red tongue, and who was festooned like an idol with pale-blue braid, maroon braid, combat ribbons, a metal stick like a whistle, the bronze star with V for valor (he was described by G.I.'s as "independent wealthy" and had imported a pool table and color TV for the men serving under him in Vietnam). Stumbling through his testimony, he apologized to the court: "I have a little trouble in the words." Yet this man, who was also deaf, felt qualified to declare that Sgt. Phu's knowledge of English was so defective that he (Kotouc) had to use signs with him.

Judge Howard's speech was surprisingly pure and precise. In the course of the trial he was the only one ever heard to use "infer" correctly ("I infer from your testimony") but also sparingly—he was more inclined to the informal "I gather from what you say." He had a nice command too of the vernacular: speaking of the lunch break, "We have problems, Mr. Bailey, getting everybody et and back." More than once, he scolded Major Eckhardt for inexact reading from a transcript, and it was probably his concern for exactitude of language (which some construed as mere fussiness) that helped one feel that he was concerned with getting at the truth. Or at least that he had *started* with that concern. About two-thirds of the way through, he seemed to give up, resign himself. Nearly every witness, leaving aside the heli-crewmen and some military character witnesses occupied with housekeeping and maintenance at various Army posts, had lied at one time or another, or, as a defense witness put it: "I've made some changes." Medina would be acquitted; the law would be satisfied, and God alone knew the larger truth.

Some of that lies or lay, certainly, in Medina's conscience. But one of the revelations that transpired from My Lai 4 was that the average American had a new conception of conscience.

It was no longer the still small voice speaking up in the night or the gnawing of remorse. When Paul Meadlo told a television audience "I had it on my conscience," he did not mean the murders he had committed. He meant the fact that some of his buddies had been killed by mines (which, by the way, seem to have been laid by South Korean "friendlies," who forgot to take them up, and not by the VC, as the men were taught). The death of his buddies preyed on Meadlo's mind and made him want to kill somebody in revenge.

Meadlo no doubt had a conscience or he would not have gone on television to half confess, half justify his part in the massacre. But in his vocabulary the word he so lamely brought out did not mean that. For him, "conscience" meant bad feelings, something akin to a bad trip. Yet perhaps in his confused soul he meant both: the bad feelings that preceded the crime and thus "caused" it and the bad feelings he got after it.

For the men of Charlie Company as heard at the Medina trial, conscience seemed to be chiefly an organ of self-justification. It did not tell you to refrain from an action but helped you explain what you did, afterward, when questioned. The witnesses talked about casualties inflicted on them by the enemy as though these were atrocities. That is, as though they themselves were *civilians*. One could hear the still-burning resentment and sense of injury in the testimony of Robert Lee, the first defense witness, as he told of a friend being cut right in half by a mine. Anybody might have thought, listening to him, that the VC should have had his friend's death on *its* conscience.

That attitude was the precipitating cause of the massacre. When a man in uniform, with a gun, makes no distinction between himself and a civilian, he will scarcely make a distinction between the military and civilians of the other side. Having been warned, furthermore, that women and children throw grenades (which happened, though not as often as pretended— too dangerous for the thrower), he will lump them all together with guerrillas, not even sorting out babies. Of course in every soldier, especially in every draftee, there is a civilian pleading for recognition, and this subjective feeling of innocent non-participation was fostered in Vietnam by U.S. propaganda, to the point where an outsider might have gathered that Gen. Westmoreland's army was some sort of UN peace-keeping agency. The illusion was encouraged by the use of terms like "pacification," "rural development," "New Life hamlets," and by Johnson's home oratory, in which he presented himself as the arch-non-belligerent.

Calley in his own trial spoke of a pre-My Lai "remorse for losing my men in the mine field, remorse that those men ever had to go to Vietnam, remorse for being in that sort of situation where you are completely helpless." In short, he felt regret for things that were not his fault, and the sad sensation, as in Meadlo's case, was presented as an excuse for mass murder, about which his conscience, so he said, was at ease. More reveal-ing, in its comedy, was his statement to a journalist: "I may be old-fashioned but I don't approve of rape on the battlefield." Calley was apologizing to the journalist for *drawing a line* some-where, that is, for still having a standard or two. He was trying to show his awareness of current permissive trends. This was typical of the killer who saw himself as a peace-movement figure.

Medina at least was more realistic. He profited from the ambiguities of the Calley outcry, which helped preclude his own conviction on the charges brought, as well as on the charge not brought. But at the time of the Peers Panel hearings, he made his position clear in a statement to the press, speaking sharply of "dissident groups in the United States that have probably welcomed the chance to talk to these people [the men of Charlie Company who were making statements to the panel]." Thus, if only for the record, he spurned an alliance with critics of the war. At the time, of course, he could not have guessed that many of those dissidents would be glad to champion him against the Army, which was getting ready to try him. Since then he has cannily stayed quiet. A little victory party was given in Bailey's suite at the Atlanta Airport Hilton to celebrate his acquittal. Eckhardt stayed away, but Wurtzel came, which gave general satisfaction as showing "the brotherly spirit of the Army." Judge Howard and his wife were present. Medina was wearing a shocking-pink shirt, white shoes, and black-and-red-striped bell-bottom trousers.

Now THAT THE CASE is closed, it does no harm to look at it, just once, from the North Vietnamese and VC point of view. Being a "backward" people, they never understood the sympathy for Lt. Calley expressed by so many war critics. For them, it did not follow that if Johnson and Gen. Westmoreland were war criminals, Calley, Medina, the two black sergeants, Meadlo, Oliver, etc. were choiceless victims of the war machine. The North Vietnamese were able to draw a line between the ordinary American soldier at Khe Sanh or Hamburger Hill shooting and being shot at by their troops and an infantry company butchering women, old men, and children. For the ordinary soldier in combat they expressed commiseration—the natural feeling that arises for another human being, whether you "approve" of him or not. But in their eyes, Medina, Calley, and company were not human beings and probably could never become so again, despite the importance given by Buddhist tradition to repentance and regeneration. No fellow-feeling could go out to them; no identification was conceivable.

Were the North Vietnamese and the NLF to win the war, they would undoubtedly try the immediate authors of the massacre, as well as Johnson, Westmoreland, Koster, and any other higher-ups they could catch—few acquittals would result. But if they could not catch Johnson and Westmoreland, they would still try and condemn all the guilty smaller fry they could lay their hands on. To act otherwise in their position would be to imply that because Hitler eluded justice by committing suicide in his bunker and Bormann and Eichmann escaped it would be *unfair* to pick on the smaller Nazis such as Ilse Koch and the lieutenants and executioners at Auschwitz.

Americans at the outset were extremely proud of having put Lt. Calley on trial, boasting that no other country would have done that, which seems true. Yet that boast was a source of anger to the local "counter-culture," which grudges this miserable country any point of pride. The plum was snatched away before it could be feasted on. Doubtless, if Calley had been acquitted, there would have been the same storm (cries of "hypocrisy," "fake justice") from the left that followed his conviction, though the right would have been appeased. The result is now visible. Medina and Henderson off the hook, Calley's sentence reduced, others not tried, several identified and unidentified mass murderers welcomed back into the population. Now any member of the armed forces in Indochina can, if he so desires, slaughter a reasonable number of babies, confident that the public will acquit him, a) because they support the war and the Army or b) because they don't.

The self-persuasion of innocence that accompanied the American soldier on the road to My Lai has its counterpart in the self-persuasion of guilt on the part of many young rebels, which they redistribute, though, to their elders and to the country at large or, more vaguely, the "system." Where the G.I. in Vietnam out on patrol felt he was really a civilian that nobody had the right to snipe at, the counter-culture is convinced that all Americans except themselves are war-makers, *i.e.*, indistinguishable from war criminals.

Such virtuous "indictments" of a whole culture in its ordinary pursuits are politically sterile. The VC and the North Vietnamese are always careful to distinguish "the American people" from "the U.S. imperialist aggressors." By the American people they mean not the proletariat (whose general support of the war they are aware of) but some larger, vaguer entity— America's better self, still found throughout the whole spectrum of classes. The assumption that everybody *has* a better self is indispensable to those working for change. The opposite assumption, of equating individuals with social categories, most of which are treated as criminal *per se*, when it does not lead to Stalinist-style mass liquidations or assassination commandos, conduces to despair and is anyway patently false. If it is not sure that everybody has a better self, history shows that nobody is totally determined by being a banker or a colonel or a hard hat.

Cynicism about "the system" is a poor guide to political action; it does not matter if the disgusted cynic is 99 per cent right in his estimates. Thus somebody like Michael Bernhardt, who did *not* write to his congressman to denounce the massacre, being too wised-up, apparently, and saturnine about results, was a wholly ineffective figure, unlike his friend Ron Ridenhour, who was naïve enough to send thirty letters, nine registered, to President Nixon, senators, and congressmen, and unlike Hugh Thompson, with his faith, partly misguided, in Major Watke. Charlie Company was well provided with cynics and reflected in an inarticulate way the contempt and hostility felt by most of the youth population toward authority. But the effect was to concur in the massacre and eventually in the cover-up, on the ground that nothing would be done anyway: the brass would see to that.

The same cynical wisdom led many American war critics to assert, in advance, that the Army, by its very nature, was incapable of trying the real criminals in the My Lai case, that Gen. Peers, being a general, was bound to play tricks with the evidence presented to his panel. . . . In short to try to deny them, through foreknowledge, any freedom of action, instead of insisting that they exercise it to the limit. The limit would scarcely have extended as far as Gen. Westmoreland, but at least he might have been demoted.

An allied notion, also dismissive of any idea of personal freedom, was voiced during the uproar following Calley's conviction: that is that Calley, somehow, was a pawn moved around from birth by "the system," which was no doubt true up to a point, but it does not follow that having failed to "make it," he was unable to tell good from evil. As though that faculty was assigned on the basis of worldly achievement or a listing in *Who's Who*; for another view, see the camel and the needle's eye. If

84

Calley's social conditioning left him no option as to whether to "open up" or not on the people of My Lai 4, then from what source did Michael Bernhardt derive his freedom to keep his rifle pointed at the ground? Where inner freedom is denied, an external force—be it only the grace of God—must govern decisions and choices, formerly thought to be made by the will. Not only do Bernhardt and those few others who refrained deserve no credit, but no blame, in the last analysis, can be assigned to anyone. Since everybody is the net result of something anterior, then (in this way of thinking), everybody is just the idle observer of his own actions. In that case, Johnson, Westmoreland, Koster, Rusk, etc. would have to be acquitted too.

Still, obviously there is a connection between higher policy and those who—let us say on their own initiative—carried out the massacre. Medina was the juncture-point, but how much he knew—or Major Calhoun, at the TOC, knew—of what was in store for the hamlet may never be found out. As has been said, the massacre was detonated by the Search-and-Destroy concept. In fact, this was not a military concept, though the military may have been persuaded that it was. The purpose of creating Free Fire Zones was not just to give the Army an open field and deprive the enemy of cover and sustenance. Behind this was a further intention, which a man of Medina's limited capacities could scarcely have guessed at and which we probably owe to Johnson's White House intellectuals.

To eliminate the ocean in which the Viet Cong fish swam required something more radical than the generation of temporary refugees, who would be housed in camps and eventually, in many cases, drift back to where their rice fields and ancestors' tombs had been. As such, the refugees were mere by-products of military operations and had no larger utility; indeed, they were more of a negative than a positive because of the pestilential conditions they were obliged to live in and the financial drain on the government of the few piasters daily given for their support. Their real usefulness was to implement what can be called a demographic solution to the war. The ultimate (or residual) aim of the Search-and-Destroy operations was to eradicate an entire rural way of life, based on a monoculture—rice—and closed off to modernization. This accounts for the systematic brick-by-brick destruction of the dwellings. The desired sequel was forced urbanization, usually an irreversible process.

By the time of My Lai 4, this was already well under way and being deplored by many Army officers, too short-sighted to see beyond the immediate problems—disease, lack of sanitation, lack of housing, corruption of morals—that the influx of homeless peasants into the cities was giving the unsteady Saigon administration. Army officers thought the people would be better resettled in New Life hamlets or whatever those were called at that period. They failed to perceive the long-run benefits, to the U.S., of a demographic shift to the cities. There the peasants, it could be hoped, would adapt to modernization, acquire cravings for consumer goods, enter light industry and commerce, acquire a service point of view. Even, some of them, get rich. The Viet Cong, a pre-capitalist agrarian phenomenon, which had its roots in the fields and in the archaic village communes, would finally fade away.

In short, forced urbanization was a nationwide version of the famous "We had to destroy the town in order to save it" pronounced during the Têt uprising. Some successes have been toted up. During the last Vietnamese election, a shift of votes to Thieu was noted, that corresponded with the shift of the population to the cities. The Viet Cong is still strong in what is left of the countryside.

Now that American main forces have largely withdrawn, Search-and-Destroy operations are no longer conducted; some of those functions have been taken over by the B-52's. But the South Vietnamese administration, picking up the slack, has embarked on its own "resettlement program." According to a Saigon dispatch of January 9, more than 1,500 persons from Quang Tri Province, described as war refugees, have been airlifted to Phoc Tuy Province, southeast of Saigon. The eventual aim, says the dispatch, is to remove 250,000 villagers from the northern provinces (still VC territory) and resettle them in the south. All of them are said to be displaced persons living in refugee camps. In the North Vietnamese version, published October 25 (and disregarded by the Americans, like the first My Lai reports, as enemy propaganda), 2,000 families from Quang Tri Province had already been removed not from camps but from their villages, and the plan calls for the relocation of 2 to 3 million peasants, who are to be forcibly sent south of Saigon from the five northern provinces. The Saigon story quoted the U.S. pacification chief and senior advisor to the South Vietnamese government: "No one's going who doesn't want to go."

As this sequel to Operation Muscatine was unfolding, soon-to-be-former Capt. Medina was appearing on the David Frost show to tell about his new job with Bailey's helicopter plant. Bailey was on the show too: "I think Ernie Medina is the right guy to stick in there to make a little company into a huge giant." Amen.

87